Logic, Cause & Action

Essays in honour of Elizabeth Anscombe

ROYAL INSTITUTE OF PHILOSOPHY SUPPLEMENT: 46

EDITED BY

Roger Teichmann

CAMBRIDGE
UNIVERSITY PRESS

PUBLISHED BY THE PRESS SYNDICATE OF THE UNIVERSITY OF CAMBRIDGE
The Pitt Building, Trumpington Street, Cambridge, CB2 1RP,
United Kingdom

CAMBRIDGE UNIVERSITY PRESS
The Edinburgh Building, Cambridge CB2 2RU, United Kingdom
40 West 20th Street, New York, NY 10011–4211, USA
10 Stamford Road, Oakleigh, Melbourne 3166, Australia

© The Royal Institute of Philosophy and the contributors 2000

Printed in the United Kingdom at the University Press, Cambridge
Typeset by Michael Heath Ltd, Reigate, Surrey

*A catalogue record for this book is available
from the British Library*

ISBN 0 521 78510 3 paperback
ISSN 1358-2461

Contents

Notes on Contributors

Elizabeth Anscombe was born in 1919. She read Greats at St. Hugh's College, Oxford, and went on to become a Research Student at Newnham College, Cambridge. While at Cambridge she attended Wittgenstein's lectures, coming to know Wittgenstein personally, and subsequently translating and editing many of his writings. She was appointed Research Fellow at Somerville College, Oxford in 1946, becoming a CUF lecturer there in 1951. She remained in Oxford until 1970, when she was appointed Professor of Philosophy at Cambridge, from which post she retired in 1986. She is the author, among other things, of *Intention* and *An Introduction to Wittgenstein's Tractatus*; most of her essays are reprinted in *Collected Philosophical Papers* (three volumes).

Nancy Cartwright is Professor of Philosophy, Logic and Scientific Method and Director of the Centre for the Philosophy of Natural and Social Science at the London School of Economics. She is author of books and articles on the philosophy of science, including *How the Laws of Physics Lie* and *Nature's Capacities and their Measurement*.

Nicholas Denyer was a student of Elizabeth Anscombe's. He is now a College Lecturer in Philosophy and Fellow of Trinity College, Cambridge, and a University Lecturer in the Faculty of Classics. He is author of various books and articles on philosophy and its history. His edition of Plato's *Alcibiades* is to be published shortly.

Michael Dummett was the Wykeham Professor of Logic at Oxford University from 1979 to 1992, and is Honorary Fellow of New College, Oxford. He is the author of books and articles on philosophy, the theory of voting, and the history of card games. He was knighted in January 1999.

Philippa Foot is Griffin Professor of Philosophy, Emeritus, University of California at Los Angeles, and Honorary Fellow of Somerville College, Oxford. Her book, *The Grammar of Goodness* and an enlarged edition of her *Virtues and Vices* will be published by OUP in 2000.

Peter Geach is married to Elizabeth Anscombe. He was Professor of Logic at Leeds University from 1966 to 1981. His writings cover logic, the history of philosophy, ethics, and more, and include *Reference and Generality*, *Logic Matters* and (with Elizabeth Anscombe) *Three Philosophers: Aristotle, Aquinas, Frege*.

Edward Harcourt is Lecturer in Philosophy at the University of Kent at Canterbury. He has published on ethics, Wittgenstein and philosophical logic. A collection of papers that he has edited, *Morality, Reflection and Ideology*, is forthcoming with OUP.

Notes on Contributors

Rosalind Hursthouse is Senior Lecturer in Philosophy at the Open University. She is the author of *Beginning Lives*, and the recently published *On Virtue Ethics* (1999). A teaching text she wrote for the Open University, *Humans and Other Animals*, will be published next year.

Stephen Makin took his PhD. at Cambridge with Elizabeth Anscombe, and teaches at Sheffield University. He is author of *Indifference Arguments*, and has published papers on Aristotelian metaphysics, Aquinas, method in ancient philosophy, and modality. He is currently completing a volume on Aristotle's *Metaphysics Theta* for the Clarendon Aristotle series.

Roger Teichmann is Lecturer in Philosophy at St. Hilda's College, Oxford. He is author of *Abstract Entities* and *The Concept of Time* (Macmillan, 1992, 1995) and a variety of journal articles, especially on logic, language and metaphysics.

Preface

One of the most striking things about the philosophical writings of Elizabeth Anscombe is their wide range – a range of which one gets some idea from the titles of the three volumes of her collected papers: *From Parmenides to Wittgenstein, Metaphysics and the Philosophy of Mind*, and *Ethics, Religion and Politics*. It is sometimes the case that a philosopher who casts his net wide sacrifices something in the way of depth. But this is the last thing that could be alleged of Anscombe's philosophy. One might almost say that depth was one of the more notorious features of her writing. Easy solutions and glib maxims are wholly absent; there is no itch to 'clinch' every argument (supplying the reader with a happy ending), nor to take up a 'position' (enabling the reader to pigeonhole the author). Sometimes this can baffle – but it is always the sort of fruitful bafflement which comes from, and in turn provokes, a real grappling with philosophical problems.

The wide range of Anscombe's work is reflected in the essays in this volume. (Her own essay, 'Making True', appears here in print for the first time.) A number of the contributors, and Anscombe herself, have connections with *Philosophy*. It was in *Philosophy* that one of the most important essays in modern moral philosophy, 'Modern Moral Philosophy', first appeared in 1958. I am very grateful to Anthony O'Hear for agreeing to publish this volume under the auspices of Philosophy and of the Royal Institute of Philosophy. The collection has been in the pipeline for some years; a few of the papers are more than a decade old. It was initially being edited by Hide Ishiguro, through the prompting of Jan Szrednicki. Acknowledgement and thanks must be extended to Professor Ishiguro for getting together four of the papers. I am grateful also to Michael Dummett and David Wiggins for their help and assistance.

Roger Teichmann

'Making true'

(Paper read to the Oxford Philosophical Society in 1982)

ELIZABETH ANSCOMBE

If you are told or otherwise believe an *either–or* proposition, the question may easily arise what makes it true. 'The potato crop in Ruritania was halved by blight in 1928' – 'Well then, either the expected, planned-for crop was in excess of the people's needs, or there was a shortage of potatoes that year, or a lot were imported. ...' That seems a fair deduction, and we may ask which was true. If only one was, then we'd say it made the disjunction true. If all were, then all of them did.

Similarly, if it is said that some elements have a certain property, the question may arise which do. Suppose someone says that iodine and chlorine do. He purports to have told us what makes the 'some' proposition true. He wouldn't be contradicted by someone who gave other ones, but not iodine and chlorine.

Thus though an *either–or* proposition or a *some* proposition, if true, must be made true by the truth of some such other proposition, in general none of these *must* be true if the original proposition is. This shows that explanation by means of truth conditions does not provide an analysis in these cases. By an 'analysis' I mean something that is at least an equivalent proposition. For an *either–or* proposition neither the conjunction of all its elements nor one of its elements nor the conjunction of any subset of its elements up to the totality of them all is a proposition equivalent to the *either–or* proposition – though any subset up to the totality will make the *either–or* proposition true. And similarly for 'some' propositions.

'The proposition is explained by giving the totality of sets of elements whose conjunction (when there is more than one) makes it true.' Or: 'It is explained by giving the totality of rows in the truth-table for its elements, for each of which it is true.' Perhaps: but the explanation gives us no equivalent. Only if you form a disjunction of the whole set will you have an equivalent. But what's the good of that, when it was the sense of a disjunction that you wanted to explain? You could go on forever in that way.

Disjunctions and propositions with 'some' are somewhat favourable examples for a concept of what makes true. In finite cases giving the totality of sets of truth-conditions gives rather precise and unexceptionable information about the sense of a proposition of this sort. If it's a 'some' proposition there is a qualification

1

to add: the case being finite, there can be a list, and when one says 'some' one is referring to the totality of sets of truth-conditions that are constructible using the list. One doesn't have to know the items which are members of the list. Neither all of them nor any of them.

However, to repeat, when one asserts a disjunction or a 'some' proposition, the question what *does* make it true is not a question about its sense. At best it may be a question about what one has in mind, a 'How d'you mean?' question. But one need not have anything in mind in that way. One may declare that someone has broken into one's desk, and have no one in mind. Similarly one may say, 'Jack or Tom or Jim did it', and not have it in mind that, e.g., Jack and Tom did.

If a disjunction is true because more than one of its elements is true, then more than one makes it true. Is this like more than one man hauling on a rope in the same direction? Each is strong enough to haul the weight that is hauled; so either they haul it quicker than either would alone, or they each have to do less work, the labour being shared. Perhaps we can answer questions about who really does the work or how much each does. But it can't be like that with two elements of a disjunction, both true. This warns us against the idea of a work done, or a force exerted, in making true. I shall return to this.

First, however, there are also other ways of making true besides the kind I have mentioned. One is to be seen in the question 'What makes *that* the French flag?' with the answer 'That it's 3 vertical stripes, that sort of width, of red, white and blue – only, by the way, it's upside down.' 'How *can* it be?' 'Sorry, I mean it's the wrong way round.' 'But then *it* isn't the French flag.'

This exchange brings out facts about flags – that you may describe them (if they aren't symmetrical about an axis parallel to the flag pole), going from the flagpole outwards.

'What makes this the French flag' is here understood to be the formal cause. But there is also a question whose answer is an historical account of the proceedings by which the French shifted from the Fleur de Lys to the tricolour. This gives us an efficient cause of this being the French flag.

There is another way of making true which is neither formal cause nor efficient cause nor fulfilment of a truth-condition. For example, the way assertions of hypocrisy are made true. I advance various facts about someone's actions, offering them as reason to call that person a hypocrite. This – taking it to be correct – is not a matter of formal cause, rather, I recount events and imply an interpretation apparently amounting to a description of hypocrisy. This

2

description would be of a formal cause – but if it in turn amounts to an efficient cause, then this efficient cause will be a cause by way of habit, not of the alleged hypocrisy, but rather of future similar hypocritical behaviour.

It isn't a formal cause because there is a step between. Hypocrisy is pretending you are virtuous in ways you are not, or pretending you lack vices which you have. Lofty condemnation of someone for a vice is implicitly a claim not to have that vice; that is the intermediate step here. Or perhaps one should rather say: Lofty condemnation of someone for, e.g., not caring for the accuracy of what he says about someone else is implicitly a claim not to go in for that sort of thing oneself. – 'Ah, but it might just be a fit of temper.' Certainly – at least certainly it can very well be a fit of temper; but the *lofty* tone of condemnation makes it not *just* a fit of temper but also a stance of righteousness. 'Well, it's all a matter of interpretation.' – That is true; but so must be any accusation of hypocrisy; and can't the interpretation be right? – 'There might be some other account to give if you knew more facts.' Possibly; but one would like that illustrated, taking the description I have started with, and applying more facts which I might reasonably be supposed ignorant of. For example, the 'lofty condemnation' was a joke, or a deliberate attempt to annoy; A was only *pretending* to have the righteous stance. Or again it was a pre-arranged signal for some non-apparent purpose. 'If I write a letter with a snarl like that in it, that's to mean that your involvement in such-and-such a fraud has been discovered and you'd better get out of the country.'

Thus we can't say we have here a 'making true' which is a matter of the formal cause. Identifying these circumstances as making the statement about hypocrisy true is identifying them as falling under a description which in turn brings them under the description 'giving a formal cause'. That is, it does so in, or given, the circumstances and on the assumption that these are all the relevant circumstances. We could say: Here, if things are what they seem, we have proceedings which make it true that A is 'rather a hypocrite'.

There are many statements which are made true in such and similar ways.

A related expression is: 'true in virtue of'. This has to be understood in the right way, not, e.g., as referring to something that *brings it about* that something is true, e.g., 'The statement was true in virtue of a verbal alteration.' Similarly it might be said that someone paid in virtue of his resolute determination to discharge all debts. But since there is no such thing as pure acts of paying, if someone paid, then he did it in virtue of, e.g., handing over some

Elizabeth Anscombe

coins, and there must always be some particular way in which he did it.

Here someone might say that 'He paid in virtue of ...' (understood in the right way) and '"He paid" was true in virtue of ...' are different. And similarly for another expression, namely, 'consisted in'. 'His paying *consisted in* his handing over some coins then' contrasts with 'The truth of "he paid" consisted in his handing over some coins then'. For the latter talks about a bit of language and the former does not. Then what about 'Its being true that he paid consisted in ...'? Now I think I need not concern myself with the *oratio recta* form – I at least would translate it into a foreign language altogether, unless there was some particular purpose for which I needed to leave the quoted bits in English. I take Q, 'Q is true', 'it is true that Q' all to be equivalent.

There is just one point to be made here, though. I might be taught to utter a sentence and told that it means such-and-such, which I hold to be true, but have forgotten everything except how to utter the sentence and that it does mean something which I hold to be true. Then I can say 'Q is true' or even 'it is true that Q' and this not be meaningless in my mouth, though Q would be. This can be explained as follows: I am saying: For some p, Q says that p, and p.

If we ask what *that* consists in, or in virtue of what it is true, or what makes it true, it seems clear that an answer would depend on what Q was – for *ex hypothesi* my utterance 'It is true that Q' can only be translated into another language leaving Q as it is. And similarly if I say 'Q is true'. For the rest, my remarks about 'some' propositions apply – even up to the possibility that there is more than one p such that: Q says that p, and p. The question falls apart: what makes it the case that Q says something? and given that it says something, i.e., that for some p it says p, what makes it the case that we can add *and p*? The first question could be answered in a rather vague way, given the information that Q was a bit of Arabic, say: for those who know Arabic it has a *use* such that for some p it says p; but we can go further only by giving (imaginary) illustrative examples, *or* by saying something that Q *does* say. This last would be like mentioning an element that did have a certain property. The second half of the question can really only be asked without total vagueness when we have got our p specified, and the questions 'what makes it the case that etc,?' about this will depend for their answer on what this p is. I may seem to have jumped a gap here – when the p is specified, what made it the case that the bit of Arabic said *that*? But that wasn't our question; our question was: what made it the case that there was something said? – and that was adequately answered by giving something that *was* said.

4

There is, then, that amount of reason to distinguish between saying that Q and saying that Q was true, or that it was true that Q. It depends on a quite particular situation. But if one can say that ..., it is all one to do so and to say that ... is true. (I leave on one side the case where '"Q" is true' is false, not because 'Q' is false, but because it lacks a truth-value because it contains a vacuous name.)

It is sometimes said that the equivalence – i.e., between p and *it is true that p* – can't be combined with a truth-condition account of meaning. The argument for this might be represented as follows:

What is the meaning of a proposition; say p?
Its meaning is given by a comprehensive account of the conditions on which it is true.
But what does 'p is true' mean?
It means the same as p.
But that's what I wanted to know in the first place, that is, what p *does* mean.

In short, if p and *it is true that p* are equivalent and you tell me conditions on which it is true that p, I don't know what you've given me conditions of, if I don't *already* know what it means to say that p. – This argument is based on a misunderstanding. You don't know till told them perhaps, either the conditions on which it is true that p, or the conditions given which, p – but they are the same. It is correct to say that, not knowing these conditions, you don't know what 'it is true that p' means (except in the sense that it, I mean p, says something which *is* so). But to say you don't know what 'it is true that p' means is the same as to say you don't know what it comes to to assert p. What you perhaps do know, or at least what is the presupposition of your question, is that there is something it comes to, and that that is the same as it comes to to assert 'p is true', and if you know the latter you know the former.

'Truth-conditions' is just a convenient locution. So 'truth-conditions of p' = 'conditions of p', that is to say: what is, or what is the range of possibility of what is, when p. Of this, there *may* be an explanation of the various kinds I've been considering – and there may not.

But in the particular case we may ask: 'What does it consist in, that ...?'.

What does it consist in, that p? – in this case? or ever?

There are plenty of cases where we know there must be an answer to the first question, and plenty where we can give some 'for example' answers to the second, though it is obvious that there isn't a complete list of possible answers which could tell what it might consist in.

But there are also cases where there doesn't seem to be an answer. For example, 'believing that there was a step there'. One has stumbled, perhaps, or nearly stumbled, at any rate trodden oddly, and one says, 'I thought there was a step there.' *When* did one think that? Obviously when one was making that step, and stepped wrong. Now does *that* mean: stepped as if for a step up, or a step down, when there wasn't one? Possibly; but has anyone ever investigated? One's reason for saying one or the other is precisely that one 'thought there was a step there', and would be able to say whether the step one thought was there was a step up or a step down. We believe that in such a case one *did* step as if for a step up, or for a step down, because it is part of one's verbal reaction (or mental description, if one merely thinks it) that one thought there was a step, and it was (say) *down*. – If one considers just what happened at the moment, inasmuch as one 'thought there was a step there', one can find nothing except the set to step down. But *that* of course will have been present at the other steps down if one was going down some steps. And that leaves out the fact that 'I thought there was a step there!' is a reaction characteristic of mis-stepping. But not of just *any* mis-stepping. We might say: that it is a characteristic reaction *defines* the special sort of mis-stepping that is in question. The reaction – the verbal reaction – doesn't have to occur; but it can still be used to define the mis-stepping. In what, then, did it consist, that 'one thought there was a step there'? We ought not to go on looking once we have realised the facts of this sort of case. That one 'thought there was a step there' belongs to a (particular kind of) mis-stepping. That is to say, the sense of it that we are considering does so. It is for example quite unlike *this* case: one passes by a narrow passage-way, and says 'I thought there was a step there but I see there isn't'.

Nor is it like the case where it looks to one as if there was a step, when there isn't, as one realises by keeping on looking. For in that case one has had the thought, or impression, 'there's a step'. But in our case one has mis-stepped, and it was *that sort* of mis-stepping and not another sort. – If one can say what deceived one, what presented the *appearance*, like a trompe l'oeil doorway, then one had the belief after the presentation. But just that is lacking in the case of simple mis-stepping, when one exclaims, 'I thought there was a step there!' It was no doubt this feature that led Russell to call this a minimal case, which furnished the minimal definition of belief as 'muscular preparedness for action'.

If what makes something true is something else – that is to say, the truth of a proposition which is not equivalent to the first – then it looks as if we had to say: 'This can't go on forever: we must come at last to the case where what makes "p" true is just that p'. Now I want to say that this is not right. If making true were like hauling, we might reasonably consider that there it must come to something that hauls without being hauled by something else – though even there we would not suppose it to haul itself, but simply to be an unhauled hauler. And the analogue would be that what makes true must itself be made true by something else, until we come to something that makes true without being made true. But making true isn't exercising a sort of force; we saw we couldn't speak of a division of labour when a disjunction was made true by the truth of all its elements. We can't ask which really does the work, or whether the disjunction is made truer, like an object being moved more quickly or further. Therefore we can't reason analogously to the argument that there must be an unhauled hauler, which is *the* hauling source of all this hauling force that is exercised. Nor is it any defence of the analogy to say that there may be more than one ultimate hauler, because if there is the force of each can be lessened or the hauling is done more quickly or a greater load is hauled.

If we did pursue the analogy while forgetting this point of contrast, then when we ascribed the truth-making to something that makes true without being made true, we should be forgetting about the other elements of the disjunction we are considering. If the truth of p consists in the truth of q or q makes it true that p, then how will we be able to accommodate the fact that it is also made true by r's being true – r being sufficient, and independent of p? Well, we *can* do so precisely because q has not done a work which must not be usurped, and can't be shared by r. But that means that the argument to the first truth-maker is not like an argument to the first, i.e., unhauled, hauler in a series of haulers each of which is hauled by its predecessors till we come to an object which hauls without being hauled.

Nevertheless, any making true must come to an end, or to several ends: a relation of making true cannot be supposed to be repeated *ad infinitum*. For if it runs in a circle, then p will be made true by q as much as it makes q true. And if it doesn't run in a circle then there never is a completed series of terms of the series. But unless we *finish* somewhere, and so indicate a finite series of terms if it doesn't run in a circle, we don't reckon to have given what makes true except in a partial way: for if r is made true by q and q by p and we simply stop at p while admitting that no doubt something else makes p true, then we have only given an incomplete account of *this* way in which r is made true. So we not merely must stop at some p, but there must be some p stopping at which finishes that particular account.

Elizabeth Anscombe

Since this is so, we must allow the termination in a proposition that makes true without being made true by something else – I mean by the truth of a non-equivalent proposition. This however does not yet give us the idea of a proposition whose truth makes true without itself being made true; for unlike hauling 'making p true' might be done by p itself. So we would have our terminus when we came to what is made true, but not by the truth of any *other* proposition. However a proposition can't make itself true: we have to gloss the statement and say 'p is made true by the *fact that* p'. If we have a Tractatus-like metaphysic of facts this would be possible: we would have reached an elementary proposition, made true by the existence of an atomic fact. But without such a metaphysic we are only saying p is made true by its being the case that p, or by its being true! That is an empty statement, with only a false air of explanation.

And so in the end we'd have to accept as termini propositions which are true without being made true. If this seems shocking, that is because of a deep metaphysical prejudice. If we take 'making true' in any of the senses that I have mentioned for it, there is no reason to be shocked. A disjunction is made true by the truth of any of its elements; but *they* don't have to be disjunctions in their turn and usually aren't. When they aren't we've got to the terminus *for that sort of making true*. There is a formal cause of this being the French flag, namely the arrangement of vertical stripes of certain colours and proportions; there may be a formal cause of the vertical but it is unlikely that it too will have a formal cause in its turn. And so the termination of truths being made true by other truths, in truths not made true in any sense that has been introduced, is not so bad after all; in fact it is altogether to be expected, or rather it is inevitable. The general principle, that what is true must be made true by something, can't be rebutted by calling in question *any* idea of making true, but it is rebutted if we demand that the particular manner of making true be given for the question that is being asked when one asks what, if anything, makes a certain proposition true.

Sentences and propositions

MICHAEL DUMMETT

Does truth attach to sentences, or to what sentences express? If to sentences, then certainly not to type sentences, such as 'I am going to London tomorrow', but only to token sentences, that is, sentences considered as uttered by a particular speaker at a particular time. It would, however, be inconvenient to restrict truth to utterances that are actually made; we may therefore adopt the device and terminology of Davidson, and speak of a 'statement' constituted by a triple $[s, i, t]$ of a type sentence s, an individual i and a time t, the existence of which does not depend on whether i in fact uttered s at t. I shall presume that the identification of a type sentence depends on identifying the language to which it belongs. A familiar, irritating obstacle prevents our explaining that, when i did not utter s at t, the 'statement' is to be said to be true just in case he would have said something true if he had done so; the obstacle consists in sentences like, 'I am not now speaking.' The difficulty is not serious. What more is needed in order to obtain, from a type sentence s, something apt to be characterised as true or false is an assignment of references to indexical and demonstrative expressions occurring in s; we may say that s 'comes out' true or false under such an assignment. We may therefore take a 'statement' $[s, i, t]$ to be true or false according as s comes out true or false under the assignment of t to the word 'now', i to the words 'I', and 'me', the place where i is at t to the word 'here', and so on. There is no reason to be disconcerted by the fact that this will yield as true a 'statement' involving the sentence, 'I have been dead for a hundred years.' Demonstrative expressions like 'that house', 'this country', etc., are less easily dealt with. Many should be regarded as devoid of reference unless, at t, i actually makes a pointing gesture or the equivalent; but the question need not be pursued here. For convenience, however, we may continue to speak of the ascription of truth to sentences, as long as we bear in mind that it is to 'statements', in our special sense, to which it is really to be ascribed.

The alternative is to treat truth as attaching to what a 'statement' expresses. This is usually called a 'proposition'. The ontological status of propositions, in the philosophical tradition, is, however, ambiguous, even when they are not identified with sentences: do they belong, in Frege's terminology, to the realm of sense or to the realm of reference? It is better to consider them as

Michael Dummett

unequivocally belonging to the realm of sense, and I shall therefore use Frege's term 'thoughts' in place of 'propositions'. A thought, if it is to be that to which truth attaches, cannot, in general, be the sense of a type sentence, for the same reason that truth cannot, in general, attach to type sentences. We accordingly need to consider a thought as involving not only the sense of a type sentence, but also a determination of the references of indexical expressions occurring in it; and there is no reason why we should not adopt the same expedient as before, taking a thought to be a triple $[s^*, i, t]$, where s^* is the sense of a type sentence, i an individual and t a time.

All the same, objections to this option are likely to be heard from philosophers who, impelled by a dread of what they call 'reification', doubt whether there are such entities as thoughts, that is, whether there are such items as senses of type sentences capable of forming constituents of triples. If we can avoid it, it is better to discuss the question without having to argue this issue. Let us therefore simply observe that the language notoriously uses 'that'-clauses in opaque contexts such as 'George believes that some fungi are poisonous', 'a proof that some fungi are poisonous', 'the hypothesis that some fungi are poisonous' and many others. An opaque context is one in which replacement of an expression by an extensionally equivalent one will not, in general, preserve truth-value: as Frege observed, its replacement by a synonymous expression *will* normally do so. Opaque contexts are perplexing, and no generally acceptable account of them has been put forward. They can, however, neither be eliminated nor dispensed with, and must therefore be explained somehow. For this reason, there can be no objection to using them to give the correct form for ascribing truth. We can accordingly reframe our question whether truth attaches to sentences or to thoughts as the question whether 'is true' is properly to be used in such a context as:

'Some fungi are poisonous' is true

or in one such as:

It is true that some fungi are poisonous,

where the 'that'-clause is understood as constituting an opaque context. In the latter case, there can now be no question of an ordered triple; rather, the references must be specified in the part of the sentence outside the 'that'-clause, as in:

It was true of John on Monday that he was going to London the next day.

For convenience, we can continue to speak of this second option as consisting in ascribing truth to thoughts, providing we do so only in ways that admit of reformulation in terms of the use of 'that'-clauses.

It may seem to go against the definition of 'opaque context' to construe the 'that'-clause in 'It is true that some fungi are poisonous' as constituting an opaque context; for the context is surely a paradigm case of a transparent one. In a sentence beginning 'It is true that ...', the replacement of an expression by an extensionally equivalent one will not alter the truth-value of the whole (unless the 'that'-clause contains some further expression inducing opacity); it appears that the 'that'-clause must constitute a transparent context. So understood, the grammatical conjunction 'that' ought not to be taken as belonging to the clause it governs, but as part of a sentential operator 'it is true that' functioning as an identity operator that maps truth on to truth and falsity on to falsity.

If, in a given context, replacement of a constituent expression by an extensionally equivalent one does not guarantee that the truth-value of the whole will be preserved, we must recognise the context as opaque. But the fact that, in a particular context, the replacement of a constituent expression by an extensionally equivalent one will always leave the truth-value of the whole unchanged does not debar us from construing that context as opaque, if there is some reason for doing so; and, in the present case, there is such a reason. Frege held that the object of a propositional attitude such as belief is a thought: if Jones believes that Tokyo is crowded, it is the thought that Tokyo is crowded that is the object of his belief. On this view, therefore, the sentences 'Jones believes the thought that Tokyo is crowded' and 'Jones believes that Tokyo is crowded' are equivalent. Frege also held that it is to thoughts that truth and falsity primarily attach, and only derivatively to sentences. The ascription of truth to the thought that Tokyo is crowded is naturally effected by the sentence 'The thought that Tokyo is crowded is true'; and it is natural to construe the sentence 'It is true that Tokyo is crowded' as effecting the very same ascription. If we so construe it, we have to take the clause that 'Tokyo is crowded' as denoting the thought that Tokyo is crowded, and hence as composing an opaque context; the fact that we are ascribing to that thought a property it shares with any thought expressed by a sentence obtained by extensionally equivalent substitutions in one expressing the thought in question does not entail that we are not after all ascribing a property to a *thought*. And, if we are ascribing a property to a thought, the clause that specifies the thought to which we are ascribing it must form an opaque context, just as it does in 'The thought that Tokyo is crowded is true' (or '... is plausible').

11

Michael Dummett

It may be objected that the argument has been viciously circular. To avoid objections to the reification of thoughts, and yet defend the possibility of taking thoughts as the subjects of ascriptions of truth-value, we appealed to sentences beginning 'It is true that ...', so construed as to take this as introducing an opaque context. Now, to defend the idea of so construing them, we have invoked Frege's thesis that it is to thoughts – which he unquestionably reified – that we ascribe truth-values. But it is illegitimate to appeal to what follows from that thesis, understood against a background according to which thoughts are taken to be objects, to vindicate a proposed means of modifying the thesis so as to dispense with that background.

We do not need to appeal to Frege's views, however, in order to make the point. The inference...:

(A) Jones believes that Tokyo is crowded
   It is true that Tokyo is crowded
   Therefore, Jones has a true belief

is unquestionably valid. It is unproblematic if, in both premises, the 'that'-clause forms an opaque context, but problematic if it forms a transparent context in the second premiss, since it indisputably forms an opaque context in the first. It may be objected that:

(B) Jones believes that Tokyo is crowded
   Tokyo is crowded
   Therefore, Jones has a true belief

is equally valid, though problematic. Its problematic character can be localised, though not, of course, dispelled, by expanding it so as to make (A) a subargument; set out in tree form, the expanded argument will take the form:

(C) Tokyo is crowded

Hence it is true that Tokyo is crowded   Jones believes that Tokyo is crowded

Therefore, Jones believes something true

where, again, the clause following 'it is true that' is taken to form an opaque context. The only problematic step is that from 'Tokyo is crowded' to 'It is true that Tokyo is crowded'; and, in all inferences that are problematic for a reason of this kind, the problem can be localised to an inference of this form, or to one of the converse form. This supplies a strong reason for construing the phrase 'it is true that' as inducing an opaque context.

This argument is not intended to establish the necessity, but only the possibility, of so understanding 'it is true that' and thereby of

12

regarding truth and falsity as ascribed to thoughts or propositions, without admitting the need to reify them. If 'it is true that' is treated as a sentential operator, then of course argument (A) is a mere variant on argument (B), and the expansion (C) pointless. The problematic character of the arguments remains: we do, legitimately, switch from a sentence in a transparent context to one containing the same sentence in an opaque context, and conversely, however this is to be explained. It is just that there is no way of localising this transition.

Now everyday usage affords us no help in choosing between the two alternatives, ascribing truth or falsity to a sentence and ascribing it to a thought, because we habitually use both idioms. This is natural, since either idiom can readily be explained in terms of the other. A true sentence is one that expresses a true thought; a true thought is one such that any sentence expressing it is true. Our question ought, therefore, to be whether it is to sentences or to thoughts that truth *primarily* attaches.

But, still, does it matter? More exactly, need there be any preferred answer? I myself have argued that it does not matter very much. I raised the question in *Frege: Philosophy of Language*, saying:

> Given that there are such things as thoughts, the issue whether it is they or sentences to which truth and falsity should be primarily ascribed seems a trivial one ... Thoughts seem intuitively the more natural choice; but, given an application of 'true' and 'false' to either, their application to the other is easily explained. (p. 370)

I then diverted the discussion to the question whether *belief* is an attitude to sentences or to thoughts, and remarked:

> But, while it is difficult to take the argument from translation seriously, it is equally difficult to take the whole issue seriously. If belief is an attitude to sentences, then the attitude of believing-true is one which has to be so understood that a man is capable of having such an attitude to a sentence which he has never heard or thought of, which he could not understand, and which belongs to a language that he does not know ... The elimination, by this means, of reference to thoughts has been accomplished at the cost of requiring us to explain such a sense of 'believes-true', etc., an explanation which will necessarily involve an account of the relation between any sentence and its equivalent within the same language, and that between it and its translation into another language. (pp. 372–3)

13

Michael Dummett

The switch of subject matter here was somewhat misleading. There is plainly a difference between believing that a sentence is true and believing the thought expressed by that sentence, where the locution 'He believes the thought expressed by "Some fungi are poisonous"' is to be taken as meaning, 'He believes that some fungi are poisonous.' One who does not understand a sentence may still have grounds for believing it to be true, though this in no way implies that he believes the thought it expresses; conversely, he may well believe that thought, without having any reason to think that particular sentence to be true. Hence if 'He believes-true the sentence "some fungi are poisonous"' is to be understood as equivalent to 'He believes that some fungi are poisonous', 'He believes-true S' cannot be interpreted as 'He believes that S is true', but must be explained in such a way as to involve the synonymy between S and other sentences, and without appealing to any feature of S not in common with those other sentences. But, for that very reason, the argument cannot be transferred from 'believes' to 'is true'. The belief held by someone who, without understanding S, believes it to be true, cannot be characterised without reference to the specific sentence S; and there are no grounds for supposing that the 'is true' which he uses in expressing his belief needs to be explained in terms of the relation of synonymy.

Naturally, someone who does understand the sentence, 'Some fungi are poisonous', will immediately conclude, from being told that the sentence is true, that some fungi are poisonous. It does not follow that it is all one whether we take the locution:

'Some fungi are poisonous' is true

or the locution:

It is true that some fungi are poisonous

as primary, still less that we can always switch from one to the other with complete insouciance.

A philosopher strongly of the opinion that there is no significant difference between the two locutions is Professor Elizabeth Anscombe. This opinion is expressed in her essay 'Making True'. She says:

Now I think I need not concern myself with the *oratio recta* form – I at least would translate it into a foreign language altogether, unless there was some particular purpose for which I needed to leave the quoted bits in English. I take Q, 'Q is true', 'It is true that Q' all to be equivalent.

The accepted mode of translating a sentence using *oratio obliqua* – a 'that'-clause – to ascribe a belief to someone was the premiss of a celebrated argument of Alonzo Church to show that belief is not an attitude to sentences but to propositions or thoughts. In *Frege: Philosophy of Language* I criticised this argument, but on the ground that the accepted canons of translation cannot be presumed to involve strict preservation of sense, as Church's argument assumes that they do (see also *The Interpretation of Frege's Philosophy*, pp. 90–1, 93–4). In support of this, I pointed out that the conventional manner of translating a sentence reporting speech in *oratio recta* was to translate the quoted speech as well, not to leave it in the original: when, in the English translation of a French history book, you read, 'Napoleon said, "Ney has blundered"', you do not suppose that Napoleon spoke in English. I was assuming that, in such a case, sense was *not* strictly preserved, since, if it were to be, the sentence quoted from Napoleon would have had to be in French. The overt content of Professor Anscombe's comment only records what she personally – and, indeed, anyone else – would normally do in translating a sentence reporting speech in *oratio recta*, which tells us nothing to the point; but there is a strong suggestion that, in so translating it, she *would* be strictly preserving sense, or else that she rejects the very notion of preserving sense.

She allows, however, that there would be exceptional cases in which she would, for a particular purpose, leave the quoted words in the original. In the next paragraph, she cites a particular type of case in which, although she did not understand a sentence Q, she might have reason to think it true, and hence might say, $\ulcorner$'Q' is true$\urcorner$. Using propositional quantification, she explains this as meaning:

For some p, Q says that p, and p.

For someone who has so far been so careful to use quasi-quotation to avoid confusing a sentence with a schematic name for a sentence, this formulation is confusing. Presumably, we are not meant to ask over what the variable 'p' ranges: this is an example of substitutional quantification, and an instantiation of the existential statement is to be obtained by replacing 'p' by a sentence.

It is unquestionably the case that, in translating from one language into another, it is usually natural to translate a word, phrase or sentence occurring, in the original, within quotation marks, but that sometimes to do so would destroy the point, or the truth, of what the original said. That is the *datum*: the problem is what a philosopher, concerned, as Professor Anscombe is, with semantic questions, ought to make of this datum. She leaves us almost entirely in the dark about what she makes of it. Does the quotation of an expression carry a different sense in cases in which the quoted

Michael Dummett

expression is to be translated from that which it carries when it would be wrong to translate it? Should we say, that is, that, in such a context as:

the two syllables of the word 'number'

the phrase:

the word 'number'

denotes something whose identity is wholly given by its phonetic and orthographic properties, but that, in contexts of a different kind, it is in effect equivalent to 'an expression having the sense (in English) of the word "number"'? Or should we say that the phrase denotes the same thing in all contexts, namely something whose identity is given by its sense as well as its phonetic and orthographic properties, but that what is said about it sometimes depends on the one and sometimes on the other? Professor Anscombe provides no clue to how she would answer these questions. Faithful to Wittgenstein's dictum that the philosopher's task consists in assembling reminders of things we perfectly well know, she simply emphasises the datum.

The question whether a sentence in quotation marks denotes something identified in part by its sense, or something identified solely by phonetic and orthographic features, seems important when we are seeking to answer the question whether truth and falsity attach to sentences or to what they express. We are left only with the knowledge that Professor Anscombe considers the three expressions:

(i) Some fungi are poisonous
(ii) 'Some fungi are poisonous' is true
(iii) It is true that some fungi are poisonous

to be equivalent. It is not, then, merely a matter of her thinking (ii) and (iii) to be equivalent, so that it is indifferent whether we ascribe truth to sentences or to thoughts: she also endorses the thesis that (i) is equivalent to both. She allows that there is *some* reason to distinguish between saying that some fungi are poisonous and saying that 'Some fungi are poisonous' is true or that it is true that some fungi are poisonous; but this 'depends on a quite particular situation' – that in which I do not understand the sentence 'Some fungi are poisonous' but have reason for believing it to be true. (Note that Professor Anscombe thinks that, even in this situation, I should be entitled to assert, 'It is true that some fungi are poisonous', as well as, '"Some fungi are poisonous" is true', i.e. that (ii) and (iii) still remain equivalent in this case. I cannot, of course, in such a case

16

assert, 'Some fungi are poisonous' not merely because I may not believe what the sentence says, but because I do not know what it says; it is absurd not to rate this an equal obstacle to my asserting, 'It is true that some fungi are poisonous.')

Professor Anscombe attacks, as based on a misunderstanding, the thesis, which I have maintained, that an explanation of what the word 'true' means solely by appeal to equivalences such as that between (i) and (ii) is incompatible with a truth-conditional theory, or, as she says, account, of meaning. Much here depends on what we take a truth-conditional theory to be, and how much we expect of an 'account'. Consider a Davidsonian truth-theory, from which we can derive 'T-sentences' of the form:

(1) 'Some fungi are poisonous' is true
    iff some fungi are poisonous.

Such a truth-theory is intended by Davidson to serve as a theory of meaning; notoriously, the word 'true' is taken as already understood. Suppose that someone proposed, as a preliminary to the truth-theory, to supply an explanation of 'true'; and suppose that he did so by means of a Tarskian truth-definition. The result of applying the truth-definition to the sentence 'Some fungi are poisonous' would be the same equivalence (1), again equating (ii) with (i). Then, having by this means specified what the term 'true' is to mean, we can use this term in the truth-theory to give the meanings of the sentences of the language: in particular, the very same equivalence (1) would now serve to explain what 'Some fungi are poisonous' means.

Such a procedure would be manifestly absurd. A complicated set of specifications would first be offered as explaining the word 'true', and then the very same set of specifications would be repeated, this time as explaining the meanings of the words and sentences of the language. It may be pointed out, however, that the absurdity does not turn on the 'homophonic' nature of the equivalences, that is, on the fact that the object-language is taken as being part of the meta-language. Suppose we have a Davidsonian truth-theory for French, formulated in English. It will yield equivalences of which the following might be a sample:

(2) 'Il y a des champignons qui sont vénéneux' is true
    iff some fungi are poisonous.

And suppose it proposed, as a prelude to this truth-theory, to explain the word 'true', as applied to sentences of French, by means of a truth-definition, formulated in English, which would, when applied to the sentence 'Il y a des champignons qui sont vénéneux', yield the very same equivalence (2). This procedure would display just the same absurdity as before: but the absurdity does not arise from there being, on the right-hand side of the biconditional, the very sentence that is referred to on the left-hand side.

Professor Anscombe's conception of a truth-conditional account of meaning is very different from Davidson's. She imagines a dialogue, which begins with the question, 'What is the meaning of a proposition, say p?'. The word 'proposition' is sometimes used for a declarative sentence and sometimes for what it expresses (a thought). But that which has a meaning is a sentence or other form of words. A thought does not have a meaning: we grasp what is meant by a declarative sentence, as uttered on a particular occasion, by grasping the thought it expresses. The questioner in the dialogue must therefore be using 'proposition' to mean 'declarative sentence'; he is using a specific (but unspecified) example, say the sentence, 'Some fungi are poisonous'.

In the dialogue, the answer is, 'Its meaning is given by giving a comprehensive account of the conditions under which it is true.' We may take it that Professor Anscombe would endorse this answer. It is clear that she understands the phrase 'truth-conditional account of meaning' as applying, not to a theory of meaning for a whole language, but to a piecemeal explanation of the meaning of a single sentence. So, thus far, we may see her as envisaging an explanation as taking the general form of a biconditional:

(3) 'Some fungi are poisonous' is true iff ...

the dots being filled by a sentence constituting a 'comprehensive account' of the appropriate condition.

The questioner now asks, 'But what does "p is true" mean?', and receives the answer, 'It means the same as p.' (Professor Anscombe shows some uncertainty whether or not she should enclose the letter 'p' in quotation marks; but, since she started without them, I am leaving them off throughout.) More specifically, if the questioner asks, 'But what does "'Some fungi are poisonous' is true" mean?', he is told, 'It means the same as "Some fungi are poisonous".' We may take Professor Anscombe as also endorsing *this* answer, which explains (ii) as being equivalent to (i).

The questioner objects that he can't understand the answer unless he already knows what 'Some fungi are poisonous' means, which is what he was enquiring after in the first place. Professor Anscombe rejects this objection as a misunderstanding. She says:

> You don't know till told them, perhaps, either the conditions on
> which it is true that p, or the conditions given which, p – but they

are the same ... to say you don't know what 'it is true that p' means is the same as to say you don't know what it comes to to assert p ... 'Truth-conditions' is just a convenient locution.

So what the second answer the questioner received invited him to do – the answer that 'p is true' means the same as p – was to substitute (i) for (ii) in the answer to his first question. The result of this is 'The meaning of "Some fungi are poisonous" is given by giving a comprehensive account of the conditions under which some fungi are poisonous.' The expression 'the conditions under which some fungi are poisonous' rings very oddly, but if we interpret it on the same lines as those on which we interpreted 'the conditions under which ... is true', the suggestion is to emend the explanatory biconditional to one of the form:

(4) Some fungi are poisonous iff ...

Now plainly Professor Anscombe cannot have it in mind to fill the dots with the very same sentence as that whose meaning was to be explained, for this would result in:

(5) Some fungi are poisonous
iff some fungi are poisonous,

which would unarguably give grounds for complaint. Plainly, she intends the dots to be filled in a more informative way, for instance thus:

(6) Some fungi are poisonous
iff there are plants without chlorophyll which
cause those who eat them to become ill or die.

And now it appears that the objection has been dispelled. It is only in stating the general principle that we need to use the word 'true'; and all we need to know about that word is that all equivalences similar to that between (i) and (ii) hold good, equivalences that will enable us to dispense with the word 'true' in applying the principle to any individual sentence.

But how can (6) constitute a way of giving the meaning of the sentence 'Some fungi are poisonous', when it does not even *mention* that sentence? The objection seems pettifoggingly pedantic. If someone, reading a book, asks me, 'What does "ombre" mean?', I may answer him by saying, 'Ombre is a three-handed card game, of Spanish origin, which was at one time immensely popular throughout Europe.' I could be regarded as trading on an explanation of 'to denote' consisting solely of a generalisation of such a specification as:

'Ombre' denotes ombre.

Michael Dummett

Using this, I have transformed the explanation '"Ombre" denotes a three-handed card game ...', which does mention the word 'ombre', in accordance with a recipe analogous to that of Professor Anscombe's for removing the word 'true'.

But, now, it would be a strange account of meaning that applied only to English sentences, and could not be extended to sentences of other languages. How, then, could we frame in English a truth-conditional account, in Professor Anscombe's sense, of the meaning of, 'Il y a des champignons qui sont vénéneux'? An initial formulation, using the word 'true', might be (2) above. To avoid using 'true', we could not here appeal to a generalisation of (1), i.e. of the equivalence between (ii) and (i). But we could appeal to a truth-definition, formulated in English, for 'true' as applied to French sentences. This, when specialised to our sentence, would yield (2) or something like it. Using this truth-definition, as Professor Anscombe would have us do, to eliminate 'true' in our statement of the truth-conditions of our sentence, we should obtain (5), or, if we were lucky, (6). But how could (5) or (6) be regarded as giving the meaning of the French sentence, 'Il y a des champignons qui sont vénéneux'? Neither of them mentions that or any other French sentence.

The obvious comment is that, while (6) does not *mention* the English sentence 'Some fungi are poisonous', it *uses* it, whereas it neither mentions nor uses the French sentence. If someone is simply ignorant of the meaning of the English sentence, (6) would certainly convey it to him (if he understood the right-hand side of the biconditional). He would not understand the biconditional, considered as an ordinary sentence, since he did not understand its left-hand side. Rather, he would apprehend that the right-hand side was intended to tell him the condition under which the left-hand side was true, or simply to give him a sentence with the same meaning as it. (6) is a perfectly good example of a means by which we may convey the meaning of a particular English sentence to someone who speaks English but does not happen to understand that sentence. But, as an explanation that will satisfy a philosopher who wishes to know what constitutes a sentence's having the meaning that it has, it is woefully deficient.

This is not a case of a sound explanation frustrated by an irritating difficulty in generalising it to other languages: it indicates a fundamental lacuna. What does someone have to know in order to know the meaning of a predicative adjective, say 'supple'? What he has to know is twofold. He must know what it is for something to be supple; or, if that is not quite the right answer, it is the answer which a truth-conditional theorist would give. We may express this first component of his knowledge as his having the concept of suppleness. But he must also know what attaches the concept to the English phrase 'is supple'. The two components of his knowledge may well be fused; he may well think of himself, quite rightly, simply as knowing what it is for the predicate 'is supple' to apply to, or be true of, something. But not only can we distinguish the two components of his knowledge: they may in fact come apart. If he comes to suffer from loss of verbal memory, he may forget the word 'supple'; but he will probably still grasp the concept, and so will continue to know what it is for something to be supple. It is just that he has forgotten how to express it briefly in English.

A philosophical account of what it is for an expression to have the meaning that it does cannot avoid referring to that expression: for it must show how the meaning attaches to the expression. It therefore cannot renounce the use of terms that serve to state how it attaches to it – terms such as 'apply to', 'denote' and 'true'. Such an account must say what someone must know in order to know what the expression means. But could we not say that an account of the kind favoured by Professor Anscombe, as illustrated by (6), encompasses the first component of the necessary knowledge? That (6), for example, displays what one must know in order to know what it is for some fungi to be poisonous? And, given this, could it not be argued that the second component can be captured by such principles as (1)? or as:

(7) 'x is supple' is true of an object a
    iff a is supple.

This could indeed be argued. The way would then be open to appeal to such an equivalence as (2), in conjunction with (6), as giving the meaning of a French sentence. But if equivalences such as (1) and (7) are to capture what a speaker knows in knowing how the meaning attaches to the sentence or expression, they cannot be regarded as laying down how terms such as 'true' and 'true of' are to be interpreted. For them to embody genuine pieces of knowledge on the speaker's part, he must be taken to understand them already: otherwise they serve only to explain terms of art that are not subsequently to be used. We may allow that 'true of' is to be explained in terms of the principles whereby a sentence is determined as true or otherwise by what the terms it contains denote, what its predicates are true of, etc.; but that does not apply to the term 'true'. It may be thought that a fully adequate account of meaning must incorporate an explanation of 'true' embodying that understanding of it according to which an equivalence like (1) may be claimed to display the second component of a speaker's knowledge of the meaning of the

Michael Dummett

sentence; or it may be contended that that is not the business of a theory of meaning. But in no case can the thesis that 'true' is to be *explained*, let alone fully explained, by equivalences such as (1) be consistently combined with a truth-conditional account of meaning.

I am certainly not myself advocating a truth-conditional account of meaning: I am deeply suspicious of the notion expressed by the phrase 'knowing what it is for ...', a notion indispensable in a truth-conditional account of understanding. My concern has been solely to show that Professor Anscombe is mistaken in maintaining that a minimalist explanation of truth is compatible with a truth-conditional account of meaning. It might be objected that she is denying something far stronger than that an *explanation* of truth by appeal to such equivalences as (1) is incompatible with a truth-conditional account of meaning, namely that, in her words, the very equivalences themselves 'can't be combined with a truth-condition account of meaning', a thesis I have never heard of anyone maintaining. But I think we must interpret her as denying the weaker claim; for it is to the answer 'It means the same as "p"' to his question 'But what does "'p' is true" mean?' that the questioner objects. He objects to the biconditional's being offered as an *explanation* of 'true': his objection makes no pretence of giving any ground for denying that the biconditional holds.

In order to achieve an explanation of the meaning of a sentence, the biconditional ought to be used in the opposite direction to that in which Professor Anscombe uses it. Instead of using (1) to eliminate the word 'true' and so transform the explanation:

(8) 'Some fungi are poisonous' is true
    iff there are plants without chlorophyll which
    cause those who eat them to become ill or die.

of the meaning of a sentence into the account (6) of the content of a thought, it should be used to introduce the word, and so transform (6) into (8). Against this, the questioner's objection would have no force, as may be seen from the following dialogue:

What is it for some fungi to be poisonous?
This is explained by giving a comprehensive account, such as (6),
    of the conditions under which some fungi are poisonous.
And what does 'Il y a des champignons qui sont vénéneux' mean?
It is true iff some fungi are poisonous.
Are you telling me what the word 'true' means when applied to
    that French sentence?
No, you idiot: I was assuming that you *knew* what 'true' means.

22

If it had been only the English sentence, 'Some fungi are poiso-nous', of whose meaning the questioner sought a clarification, he would have rested content with the answer to his first question; for he would have known that (1) held good, and would have tacitly used it to transform (6) into (8). But, in so using (1), he would not have been treating it as a (partial) *definition* of 'true'; for to do so would have yielded no understanding of the sentence.

(8) can be dissected into (6) and (1), representing the two compo-nents of understanding; but no more than before can (1) be regard-ed as *explaining* 'true', since it still represents a speaker's grasp of what 'Some fungi are poisonous' expresses. Although the two com-ponents can come apart, a speaker's understanding is not normally a conjunction of two separate pieces of knowledge he has had to acquire – his grasp of the sense that a sentence in fact expresses, and his knowledge that it is the.sense of that sentence. Rather, he prob-ably came to grasp the thought by coming to understand that sen-tence or some other that expresses it. Even if he already grasped the thought before he came to understand the sentence, his coming to understand it was not achieved by his attaching that already famil-iar thought to the sentence: rather, having come to understand the sentence, he then recognised it as expressing a thought already familiar to him. For this reason, the undissected (8) gives a better representation of the meaning of the sentence than the combination of (6) and (1). Not, indeed, a very good representation, from the standpoint of one seeking a correct philosophical account of a speaker's understanding of his language; but we need not explore the matter further. A truth-conditional theory of meaning of the kind that I have elsewhere called a 'modest' one attempts only to capture the second of the two notional components of meaning; Professor Anscombe's conception of a truth-conditional account of meaning at best captures only the first. Neither can be omitted from an adequate account; and neither can appeal to a minimalist expla-nation of truth. Professor Anscombe was indeed concerned with a misunderstanding; but the misunderstanding was hers.

The first person: problems of sense and reference

EDWARD HARCOURT

0 Consider 'I' as used by a given speaker and some ordinary proper name of that speaker: are these two coreferential singular terms which differ in Fregean sense? If they could be shown to be so, we might be able to explain the logical and epistemological peculiarities of 'I' by appeal to its special sense and yet feel no temptation to think of its reference as anything more exotic than a human being. But if 'I' as used by a given speaker and an ordinary proper name of that speaker are to be related as Fregean theory would have it, at least two things must be true. First, there must be something like a mode of presentation of the speaker which 'I' expresses; and secondly, what 'I' expresses on the lips of a given speaker must be something which would vary as the reference of 'I' varies. However, if the first condition is not fulfilled – if 'I' does not express anything *like* a mode of presentation of the speaker who utters it, not even something that is constant from speaker to speaker – then there is no point in asking about the second condition: a Fregean account of 'I' can already be ruled out. The question this paper addresses is whether 'I' can be said to express anything like a Fregean mode of presentation of its referent, and the conclusion is that it cannot.

The paper proceeds by offering a commentary on Elizabeth Anscombe's 'The First Person'.[1] 'The First Person' is best known, however, not for any thesis about the *sense* of 'I', but for what we may call the 'no reference' thesis, the thesis that 'I' is 'neither a name nor another kind of expression whose logical role is to make a reference, *at all*'.[2] If that thesis is true, then 'I' as used by a given speaker and an ordinary proper name of that speaker evidently cannot be related as two coreferential singular terms which differ in Fregean sense, or indeed in sense understood in some liberalised non-Fregean way. The strategy of the paper, then, is as follows. Anscombe argues for the no reference thesis by *reductio*. In the first part of the paper (sections 1–4), I argue that the *reductio*'s intended

[1] In G. E. M. Anscombe, *Collected Philosophical Papers vol. II: Metaphysics and the Philosophy of Mind* (Oxford: Blackwell, 1981), pp 21–36.

[2] 'The First Person', p. 32. Cf. ibid., p. 31: '["I" is not] a word whose role it is to "make a singular reference"'.

25

conclusion – the no reference thesis itself – cannot be right. Either it is a thesis which has consequences for the logical form of first person sentences, or it is not, and is based instead on a non-standard definition of the term 'referring expression'. If the former, then the thesis must be rejected because those consequences are false. If the latter, the thesis stands or falls with the non-standard definition, and the definition seems ill-grounded. In the second part of the paper (sections 5–8), I ask what is left of the *reductio* argument given that its conclusion is false. I defend the argument against some recent criticism and argue that the *reductio* would work *if* one were to accept Anscombe's non-standard definition of 'referring expression'. But if this conditional claim is true, then although Anscombe's non-standard definition should not be accepted, the *reductio* turns out to be a good argument not for the no reference thesis but for a valuable conclusion about the kind of understanding we have of 'I', namely that 'I' is not associated with any 'conception', or mode of presentation, of an object. Independently of the no reference thesis, therefore, 'I' and a proper name of the person who utters it cannot be related as two coreferential singular terms associated with different Fregean senses. However, the notion of sense may also be taken more liberally, as the content of a competent speaker's understanding whether or not that understanding involves association with a mode of presentation. And to show that 'I' and a proper name of the person who utters it are coreferential singular terms which are differently understood, i.e. which differ in sense on this liberalised view of the notion, surely clears the way for a metaphysically palatable explanation of the peculiarities of 'I' as effectively as a more standard Fregean account.

1 Whatever else it is, the no reference thesis is a thesis about the semantic category to which 'I' should be assigned. The thesis is also completely general. It resembles a thought of Wittgenstein's from the 1930s: in the *Blue Book*, for example, Wittgenstein distinguishes between two uses of 'I', the 'use as subject' and the 'use as object',[3] and claims that in the former but not the latter, 'I' neither 'denote[s] a particular body' nor makes 'statement[s] *about* a particular person'.[4] There is no evidence, however, that Anscombe herself

[3] L. Wittgenstein, *The Blue Book* (Oxford: Blackwell, 1978), p. 66.
[4] *The Blue Book*, pp. 67, 74. See also G. E. Moore, 'Wittgenstein's Lectures in 1930–33', *Mind* 64 (1955), where Moore reports Wittgenstein as saying that in 'I have a match-box' and 'Skinner has a match-box', '"I have..." and "Skinner has ..." really [are] values of the same propositional function', but 'in the case of "I have tooth-ache" ... the use of "I" is utterly different' (p. 14).

intends her thesis to apply to anything less than *all* uses of the first person pronoun.[5] And, since it is at best unnatural to treat 'I' as systematically ambiguous between different types of use, this is a virtue of Anscombe's thesis as compared to the *Blue Book* version.

Now for many, it is sufficient for an expression to belong to the semantic category of referring expressions that it have a certain logical syntax, i.e., that sentences in which it occurs stand in certain inferential relations to other sentences and that it contribute to the truth-conditions of the former sentences in a certain systematic way. Let us call satisfaction of these two conditions together 'the normal test' for referring expressionhood. It is precisely because Anscombe has been understood to agree that the normal test is the *right* test that her thesis has sometimes been greeted with amazement,[6] since it certainly *seems* as if 'I' passes the test.

Curiously, however, Anscombe herself concedes what on the view

---

[5] P. M. S. Hacker (*Wittgenstein: Meaning and Mind: An Analytical Commentary on the* Philosophical Investigations, vol. III (Oxford: Blackwell, 1990)) cites the following two passages from Wittgenstein's later Nachlass which show that the completely general no reference thesis also has a Wittgensteinian ancestry. (1) 'It is correct, though paradoxical, to say: "I" does not refer to [bezeichnet] a person' (from MS 116, p. 230, cited in Hacker, *Wittgenstein*, p. 487); and (2) '"Ich" in meinem Munde bezeichnet *mich*.' Bezeichnet denn dieses Wort in meinem Munde etwas besonderes? Ich wollte wohl sagen: '"Ich" bezeichnet immer den Mensch [sic] der es ausspricht.' Aber was heisst das, es bezeichne ihn? Gibt es denn da nur *eine* Möglichkeit?' ('"I" on my lips refers to *me*.' So does this word on my lips refer to something special? I *wanted* to say: '"I" always refers to the person who utters it'. But what does it mean, it refers to him? Is there only *one* possibility here?" (my translation). From MS 120, p. 230, cited in Hacker, *Wittgenstein*, p. 488.) In both cases, and especially the second, the thesis is advanced rather tentatively. Moreover it does not find its way into the *Philosophical Investigations*. Its nearest equivalent there is '"I" is not the name of a person, nor "here" of a place, and "this" is not a name' (section 410). But since Wittgenstein's use of 'name' here excludes demonstratives while Anscombe's includes it, this passage cannot be taken as an expression of the no reference thesis. Indeed a passing comparison in *On Certainty* (eds G. E. M. Anscombe and G. H. von Wright, trans D. Paul and G. E. M. Anscombe (Oxford: Blackwell, 1979)) suggests that Wittgenstein may have come to think of 'I' in a much more 'Fregean' way: 'To think that different states must correspond to the words "believe" and "know" would be as if one believed that different people had to correspond to the word "I" and the name "Ludwig", because the concepts are different' (section 42).

[6] See for example Gareth Evans, *The Varieties of Reference* (Oxford: Clarendon Press, 1982), p. 212, note 14.

of referring expressionhood defined by the normal test appears to be quite enough to defeat her thesis. Thus for example she says that 'we haven't got [the sense of "I"] just by being told which object a man will be speaking of, whether he knows it or not, when he says "I"'.[7] This implies that, when a man says 'I', he will be *speaking of* an object, and the notion of speaking of an object does not seem very far removed from that of *referring to* it. More strikingly, she says that 'I' 'functions syntactically like a name',[8] that '[i]f X asserts something with "I" as subject, his assertion will be true if and only if what he asserts is true of X',[9] and thus that 'I' 'can be replaced *salva veritate* by a ... name of X when it occurs in subject position in assertions made by X'.[10] These concessions sow the suspicion that, when it is properly understood, Anscombe's thesis is not really so controversial after all, and that Anscombe advanced it not because she thought (for whatever reason) that 'I' fails the normal test but because she took a different view of the criteria for assigning expressions to semantic categories in general, or to the category of referring expression in particular.[11]

The arguments which Anscombe advances for her thesis add to this suspicion. She argues – though she does not put it quite like this – that expressions divide into semantic categories according to the kind of knowledge required for their correct use. And if an expression is to belong to the category of expressions 'whose logical role is to make a reference', this knowledge must at least include posses-

---

[7] 'The First Person', p. 23.

[8] Ibid.; see also Anscombe, *Collected Philosophical Papers*, vol. II, pp. 24, 29–30.

[9] Anscombe, *Collected Philosophical Papers*, vol. II, pp. 32–3; see also p. 29.

[10] Anscombe, *Collected Philosophical Papers*, vol. II, pp. 29–30.

[11] Cf. Anscombe's claim that 'I am E[lizabeth] A[nscombe]' is 'not an identity proposition' ('The First Person', p. 33). If that means that 'I am EA' does not have a logical form in common with, say, 'Hesperus is Phosphorus', Anscombe is right to regard the claim as required by the no reference thesis on the assumption of the normal test for referring expressionhood. Anscombe wisely does not deny, however, that 'EA is illegally parked' and 'I am EA' jointly imply 'I am illegally parked'. But she must deny that the inference depends on a substitution on the basis of identity, so what *is* its structure? Perhaps the inference is *sui generis* because it involves 'I'. But that fact would only be a reason to deny that the pattern is the same as in 'Hesperus is bright, Hesperus is Phosphorus, so Phosphorus is bright' if it had *already* been shown that 'I' is not a referring expression. As this has not yet been shown, the suspicion is once again that Anscombe's apparently controversial claim does not after all concern the logical form of 'I am EA', and is based instead on a non-standard definition of 'identity proposition' corresponding to a similar definition of 'referring expression'.

sion of a '"conception" through which [the expression] attaches to its object'.[12]

'Conception' is an Anscombean term of art and requires some explanation. In Anscombe's view, to specify a '"conception" through which an expression attaches to its object' would be to specify for the expression a way its referent is 'reached' by one who uses it, 'what Frege called an "Art des Gegebenseins"'.[13] So at a general level, a 'conception' is Anscombe's interpretation of Frege's notion of a mode of presentation of an object. More specifically, an Anscombean 'conception' is a concept under which the referent of a referring expression falls, a concept of the kind of thing it is. Anscombe writes:

> If 'I' is supposed to stand for its object as a proper name does, we need an account of a certain kind. The use of a name for an object is connected with a conception of that object. And so we are driven to look for something that, for each 'I'-user, will be the conception related to the supposed name 'I', as the conception of a city is to the names 'London' and 'Chicago', that of a river to 'Thames' and 'Nile', that of a man to 'John' and 'Pat'.[14]

The thought here – which seems exactly right – is that the comprehending use of a proper name for an object requires one at least to be able to grasp the difference between using the name correctly and using it incorrectly. To use a name incorrectly is to apply it, on a given occasion, to some object distinct from the object to which it in fact applies. So its comprehending use requires one to know whatever one needs to know in order to understand an identity-statement one of whose relata is the name in question. (I do *not* say that one actually needs the wherewithal to judge such an identity-statement to be true.) But, on a plausible view of identity, understanding an identity-statement requires mastery of a certain sort of concept, a concept of the kind of thing to which the referent of the name belongs.[15] So comprehending use of a proper name requires grasp of an Anscombean 'conception'.

Now it may look as if the test of association with a conception is meant to apply to 'I' only on the assumption that, as used by a given

---

[12] Anscombe, *Collected Philosophical Papers*, vol. II, p. 29. It should be noted that the context-sensitivity of 'I' plays no part in Anscombe's argument.

[13] Anscombe, *Collected Philosophical Papers*, vol. II, p. 23.

[14] Anscombe, *Collected Philosophical Papers*, vol. II, p. 26.

[15] For statements of this kind of view, see, e.g., David Wiggins, *Sameness and Substance* (Oxford: Blackwell, 1980), chs. 2 and 3, and Dummett, *Frege: Philosophy of Language* (2nd edition, London: Duckworth, 1981), ch. 16.

Edward Harcourt

speaker, it is a proper name of that speaker. But the demand for a conception is meant to carry over to demonstratives too: Anscombe says that a speaker needs to be able to answer the question 'this what?' if he is to be meaning anything by 'this', and to answer 'this what?' would be to supply a 'conception of the object indicated'.[16] Now one can ask (pointing, for example, to an unfamiliar lump in the plasterwork) 'what's this?' without already knowing any more about the kind of thing it is than simply that it is a lump. But as long as the criteria of identity carried by a conception are allowed, in some cases, to be fairly weak, Anscombe's claim seems right.

Finally, Anscombe says that 'I' would have to be if not either a name or a demonstrative then a disguised definite description if it was a referring expression at all. So, since definite descriptions evidently express a conception of the thing (if any) which satisfies them, the requirement for a conception can be treated as Anscombe's test for membership of the class of referring expressions generally. But, she argues, no such conception can without absurdity be specified for 'I'. Moreover a description of the use which 'I' *does* have shows that the knowledge required for it is of quite a different sort. So 'I' does not belong to the semantic category of referring expressions.[17]

I will return to these arguments in more detail later. For the moment, we need notice only that they are epistemological, and thus liable to raise the protest that epistemology is one thing, semantics another. Why, it may be objected, should the fact that a conception of the appropriate sort cannot be specified for 'I' – interesting as it may be – decide the semantic category to which 'I' belongs, while facts about the logical syntax of first person sentences do not? The general question of the relation between semantics and epistemology, and therefore the question how the category of referring expression is best to be defined, is not a merely verbal one. But unless Anscombe's position on this general question has controversial consequences for the logical syntax of 'I' as defined by the normal test, it looks as if any disagreement about the semantic category to which 'I' belongs can be avoided by switching one's definition of 'referring expression'. And, given the concessions already noted, it is hard to see what further such controversial consequences Anscombe's epistemological claims could have.

[16] 'The First Person', p. 27.

[17] Again on p. 23, the argument is that it is impossible to specify a way in which the purported referent of 'I' is 'reached' by one who uses the expression, so 'I' is not a referring expression.

The first person: problems of sense and reference

2 It would be strange, however, if Anscombe *did* straightforwardly intend her thesis in such a way that it could be sidestepped by relabelling. So let us assume that Anscombe accepts the normal test for referring expressionhood, and thus give the idea that the no reference thesis does have consequences for the logical form of first person sentences a fair hearing.

If there is to be room for Anscombe to deny something about 'I' which the normal test for referring expressionhood apparently requires us to assert, the concessions noted above cannot be taken as concessions about the *logical* syntax of 'I'. On the contrary, if they are to be compatible with the claim that the logical syntax of 'I' differs from the logical syntax characteristic of a referring expression, they can be no more than concessions about its *surface* syntax.

That Anscombe intended the concessions only in this way is supported by her identification of a 'conception' with a Fregean mode of presentation of an object. For then it looks as if to claim that no such conception can be specified for 'I' is to claim that 'I' does not express the kind of sense that is characteristic of a Fregean *Eigenname*, and to claim that is to make a claim about the logical syntax of 'I'. Further evidence that Anscombe intends the no reference thesis as a thesis about the logical syntax of 'I' comes out in the use she makes of William James's story of 'Baldy', who falls out of a carriage and then asks '"Did anyone fall out?" or "Who fell out?"'.[18] Baldy's question, according to Anscombe, shows that 'his thought of the happening, falling out of the carriage, was one which looked for a subject, his grasp of it one which required a subject'. Baldy's grasp of his question, in other words, shows that it contains the one-place predicate 'x fell out', just as the sentence 'Someone ate this porridge, but I don't know who' contains the predicate 'x ate this porridge'. But in this, Baldy's grasp of his question is, according to Anscombe, precisely unlike a normal person's grasp of 'I fell out'. For the latter does 'not involve the connection of what is understood by a predicate with a distinctly conceived subject',[19] and therefore (apparently) does *not* contain the one-place predicate 'x fell out'. Now if 'I fell out' does not contain the one-place predicate 'x fell out', then it looks as if there can be no logical structure to be discerned within it at all. So while it would share a logical form with the no-place 'it's raining', it would not share a logical form with 'Goldilocks ate this porridge'. This is evidently a claim about the logical syntax of 'I' and one which, if true, would show that 'I' failed the normal test for referring expressionhood.

[18] 'The First Person', p. 36. See William James, *The Principles of Psychology* (2 vols., London: Macmillan, 1891), vol. I, p. 273n.
[19] 'The First Person', p. 36.

31

In this light, let us consider again Anscombe's concession that 'I am F' as said by X is true iff X is F. Her reasons for saying that this does not show that 'I' is a referring expression are as follows:

> One who hears or reads a statement with 'I' as subject needs to know whose statement it is if he wants to know of whom the predicate holds if the statement is true. Now, this requirement could be signalled by flashing a green light, say, in connection with the predicate, or perhaps adding a terminal '−O' to it. ... What would make such a signal or suffix into a referring expression? The essential argument cannot be an argument back from syntax to reference, for such an argument would depend only on the form of the sentence and would be absurd. (E.g. no one thinks that 'it is raining' contains a referring expression, 'it'.)[20]

And it *would* of course be wrong to argue that 'I' is a referring expression just because it can stand as the grammatical subject of a singular verb, since the same argument 'from syntax to reference' would licence the same conclusion about the 'it' in 'it's raining'. A 'logician' who argued on this basis to the conclusion that 'I' is a referring expression would be insensitive indeed.[21]

Again in defence of the view that 'I' has the syntax of a referring expression only superficially, Anscombe claims that 'the truth-condition for the whole sentence does not determine the meaning of the items within the sentence'.[22] But while this is true enough, it is also irrelevant here. For as Anscombe would herself agree, even the contribution made to the truth-condition of the sentence by a *particular item* within it is not enough to determine the *meaning* of that item: 'as Frege held, there is no path back from reference to sense'.[23] I assume therefore that Anscombe meant to appeal not to the principle that the truth-condition of the whole does not determine the meaning of each part, but rather to the (no less true) principle that the truth-condition of the whole does not determine the way any of the parts contributes to it. Thus, though a given utterance of 'it is raining' is true if and only if rain is falling in a particular place at a particular time, the 'it' makes no distinctive contribution to the utterance's having that truth-condition. Similarly, it is not possible

[20] Ibid., p. 30.

[21] For the character of the 'insensitive logician', see Anscombe, 'The Subjectivity of Sensation', *Collected Philosophical Papers vol. II: Metaphysics and the Philosophy of Mind*, p. 55. Cf. also 'The First Person', p. 24: 'Certainly to the eyes of our logicians ["I"] is a proper name. Are their eyes dim?'.

[22] 'The First Person', p. 33.

[23] Ibid., p. 23.

to read off the manner in which 'I' contributes to the truth-condition of 'I am F' as said by X, if it contributes at all, from the bare fact that 'I am F' as said by X is true iff X is F.

However, the above considerations do not show that 'I' is *not* a referring expression but only that the no reference thesis, understood as a thesis about logical syntax, is *consistent* with first person sentences having the surface syntax and truth-conditions which they in fact have. We now need to ask whether it is *true* that 'I' does not have the logical syntax of a referring expression as defined by the normal test.

The idea soon runs into difficulties. In conformity with the generality of the no reference thesis, Anscombe does not distinguish between one use of 'I' in which first person sentences are no-place predicates and another use in which they are analysable into a one-place predicate and a singular term. This leaves Anscombe with a more pervasive form of a problem which confronts the *Blue Book* Wittgenstein. If 'Jones is sitting down' *does* contain the predicate 'x is sitting down', as it surely does, then it looks as if when Jones says 'I am sitting down', he does not predicate of himself what another would predicate of him by using the words 'Jones is sitting down'. That predicates are ambiguous as between their first and third person uses is a hard enough conclusion to swallow even when, as with psychological predicates, there are special facts such as the first/third person asymmetry of psychological ascriptions to call in aid to explain it. But in the present case there are no such special facts.

Anscombe could perhaps reply that for two people to employ the same predicate does not require them to utter sentences which have the same logical form. But given the truth-conditional contribution and inferential role of 'I', why deny that the one-place 'x is sitting down' occurs in Jones's 'I am sitting down'? First, the contribution made by 'I' to the truth-condition of a sentence in which it occurs is unlike that made by 'it' in 'it's raining'. In the latter case the truth-conditional contribution is nil: 'it' does no more than ensure the grammaticality of the sentence. But this is precisely not true of 'I'. The subject-term of 'I fell out' tells us which *object* must satisfy the property expressed by the predicate if the sentence (on a particular occasion of utterance) is to be true. The way in which the subject-term of the sentence contributes to the truth-condition of the whole is, in fact, precisely the manner one would expect of a 'logically proper name'.

Exactly the same is true of 'I' on the score of inferential relations to other sentences. Though 'it's raining' does not entail 'something is raining', 'I am in pain' *does* entail 'someone is in pain'; and in case someone tries to argue that although *another* person can draw this consequence from an utterance by me of 'I am in pain', the consequence somehow does not follow *for me*, one need only consider the fact that I can contradict another's statement 'it is not the case that anyone in the room is in pain' by saying 'I am in pain', if I am in the room.[24] Similarly, someone who reads the sentence 'Anyone who is under 18 and born in the Channel Islands is eligible for a scholarship' can infer 'I am eligible for a scholarship', if that person also knows that he is under 18 and born in the Channel Islands; and from these same pieces of knowledge, he can infer 'there is at least one person who is under 18 and born in the Channel Islands'. 'I' passes a great many tests for referring expressionhood with reference to the inference-patterns of ordinary English with flying colours.[25]

3 In search of a feature of the logical syntax of 'I' which might yet provide a reason for denying that it is a referring expression as defined by the normal test, I want to consider briefly one more type of case, that of indirect contexts. Following some proposals by Geach and Castañeda,[26] an argument for the no reference thesis based on indirect contexts might be constructed as follows. Suppose that:

(1) Smith believes that Jones is a famous author

entails:

(2) There is someone such that Smith believes that he is a famous author.

Suppose also that the indirect reflexive 'he', used to report a first person utterance or to attribute a propositional attitude which the

[24] The idea that (at least some) first person sentences are no-place predicates (as on Anscombe's account) for the utterer but not for the hearer is to be found in C. J. F. Williams, 'Myself', *Ratio* (New Series) 4 (June 1991), p. 82. His main argument for this claim is epistemological, namely that my utterance of 'I am in pain' does not require me to identify any object as satisfying the predicate, though the attribution of pain to me by another would do so ('to this epistemological asymmetry there corresponds a syntactical asymmetry').

[25] An array of such tests is set out by Dummett, *The Interpretation of Frege's Philosophy*, pp. 59ff, and in Crispin Wright, *Frege's Conception of Numbers as Objects* (Aberdeen University Press, 1983), pp. 53ff.

[26] See P. T. Geach, 'On Beliefs About Oneself', pp. 128–9, and H.-N. Castañeda, '"He": A Study in the Logic of Self-Consciousness', *Ratio,* 8 (1966), pp. 130–57.

subject would express by means of such an utterance, is logically speaking the same expression as 'I'.[27] Thus if 'I' were, like 'Jones', a referring expression, then:

(3) Smith believes that he is being persecuted by aliens

would entail:

(4) There is someone such that Smith believes that he is being persecuted by aliens,

where the 'he' in (3) is the indirect reflexive while the 'he' in (4) is an ordinary anaphoric pronoun. But (so the argument runs) the entailment from (3) to (4) does not hold, so 'I' is not a referring expression.[28]

What are we to make of this argument? It is controversial whether there is a general licence to infer sentences of the form 'There is someone such that *a* believes that he is F' from belief-attributions to *a* which embed a singular term: Smith might believe that Zeus is the cause of thunder, but it does not look as if this implies the existence of Zeus. And if there is no such general licence, the invalidity of the inference from (3) to (4) shows nothing special about the indirect reflexive, or therefore about 'I'. But it might be replied that, just because 'Zeus' is empty, it is not a singular term at all, and thus no counterexample to the view that inferences such as that from (1) to (2) are valid. So let us see what can be made of the argument on the assumption that the inference from (1) to (2) is in order.

The justification for allowing the inference from (1) to (2) but disallowing that from (3) to (4) seems to be the following. If one can say 'There is someone such that Smith believes he is F' then one should be able to ask 'who?'. In the case of (1), the answer to this

[27] For a defence of this assumption, see, e.g., J. E. J. Altham, 'Indirect Reflexives and Indirect Speech', in Cora Diamond and Jenny Teichman (eds), *Intention and Intentionality*, (Brighton: Harvester Press, 1979), pp. 25–38.

[28] For the denial of the entailment from 'The Editor of *Soul* thinks that he* is rich' to 'The Editor of Soul thinks that the Editor of *Soul* is rich', see H.-N. Castañeda, '"He": A Study in the Logic of Self-Consciousness', pp. 134–5. If the second sentence is construed as 'The Editor of *Soul* thinks that there is just one person who is Editor of *Soul* and that person is rich', then the entailment indeed does *not* hold. But Castañeda also denies the entailment where the second sentence is read as 'There is just one person who is Editor of *Soul* and the Editor of *Soul* thinks that that person is rich', and the latter denial – reformulated so as to be independent of special facts about definite descriptions – is what is at issue here.

question is 'Jones', a free-standing unit of sense and a singular term. With (3), by contrast, the question can be answered only by 'himself'. But this is not even a free-standing unit of sense: to give this answer is simply to repeat a fragment of the 'that'-clause of the original belief-attribution. But only where the answer to the 'who (or what)?' question is a free-standing unit of sense and a singular term are statements of the form 'There is someone (something) ...' really in order. So we cannot move from (3) to (4).

In reply, let us make the (disputed but hardly outlandish) assumption that co-referential singular terms can differ in sense. On this assumption, though Hesperus is Phosphorus, it does not follow that if *a* believes that Hesperus is bright, *a* believes that Phosphorus is bright. Now suppose, as the argument has it, that 'Smith believes that Hesperus is bright' entails 'There is something such that Smith believes that it is bright'. We can then ask 'what?' Now if the point of the answer is simply to introduce an object, then it cannot matter how we introduce it, so we commit no error if we answer 'Phosphorus'. However, 'There is something such that Smith believes that it is bright' and 'The thing such that Smith believes that it is bright is Phosphorus' jointly entail 'Smith believes that Phosphorus is bright'. But, on the assumption that coreferential singular terms can differ in sense, that is apparently *not* entailed by 'Smith believes that Hesperus is bright'.

There seem to be two ways round this problem. Either the 'who or what?' question must be taken in such a way that it may only be answered by quoting back a fragment of the 'that'-clause in the original belief-attribution, or else 'Smith believes that Phosphorus is bright' must be taken in a sense which makes no claim to be fully specific as to the content of Smith's belief (as it is sometimes put, 'Smith believes, of Phosphorus, that it is bright').

Neither tactic is much help to the defender of the no reference thesis. If we take the first option, then the fact that in answering 'himself' to the question 'Who is such that Smith believes that he is being persecuted by aliens?' we do no more than quote back a fragment of the original belief-attribution does not prove any disanalogy between the indirect reflexive and 'Jones' or 'Hesperus'. For we have seen that there is *a* sense of the 'who or what?' question even in the 'Hesperus' case where we will answer incorrectly if we do more than that. But 'Hesperus' is obviously a referring expression, so (carrying on the assumption, required by the argument under examination, that the indirect reflexive is logically speaking the same expression as 'I') we have not yet found a reason to deny this of 'I'.

If we take the second option, the question is whether, when (3) is true, we are allowed to say, by analogy with the Hesperus case, that Smith believes of Smith that he is being persecuted by aliens – again making no claim to be fully specific as to the content of Smith's belief. Now if 'I' is the same, logically speaking, as the indirect reflexive and 'I' is *not* a referring expression, then when Smith (expressing his belief) says 'I am being persecuted by aliens' he is not referring to the person he is, i.e. Smith; and, if that is so, then perhaps he has not said that the predicate 'x is being persecuted by aliens' holds of that person. But even if all that is true, the argument runs in the wrong direction. The no reference thesis is being used to support the claim that one cannot infer (4) (in the sense of 'Smith believes, of Smith, that he is being persecuted by aliens') from (3). But what was needed was some fresh reason, deriving from the case of indirect contexts, to support the no reference thesis. Either way, consideration of indirect contexts in general and of the indirect reflexive in particular gives us no new reason to accept the no reference thesis.

4 In summary, if the thesis that 'I' is not a referring expression uses 'referring expression' as defined by the normal test, then it implies differences in logical syntax between 'I' and paradigmatic referring expressions. But the differences needed to establish the thesis do not exist. So let us turn to the second alternative I envisaged in section 0, that the thesis is not intended to imply any such differences and is based instead on a non-standard way of delimiting the class of referring expressions. Though the thesis would then be less radical, none of the foregoing arguments would count against it. Is the thesis tenable when understood in this more modest way?

So understood, the 'no reference' thesis is only as good as the non-standard definition of 'referring expression' on which it is based, and if expressions are *not* to be assigned to semantic categories according to the kind of knowledge required for their correct use, the non-standard definition is unacceptable. But the non-standard definition, and thus the no reference thesis, is unacceptable even if this is the right approach to semantic categories. In a review of Evans's *The Varieties of Reference*, Geach attributes three theses to Anscombe in 'The First Person': that 'I' is not a multiply ambiguous proper name like 'Smith', that it is not to be assimilated to a demonstrative, and that it does not abbreviate a definite description.[29] If one accepts these theses and yet maintains that 'I' is a 'referring expression', he says, this would be as pointless as maintaining that 'a cat of nine tails and a Manx cat are two varieties

[29] *Philosophy* 61 (Oct. 1986), pp. 534–40.

of cat, differing in the number of tails'.[30] However, 'I' shares its logical syntax with 'Smith' and (arguably) with demonstratives, and this common property is scarcely trivial or accidental, or based on equivocation.[31] Nor can one defend the refusal to classify 'I' as a referring expression by appeal to the idea that referring expression-hood is an epistemological category. Of course if the entry condition for that category is association with a conception, as explained above, the category is indeed an epistemological one, i.e., a category based on the kind of knowledge required for an expression's correct use. But it does not follow from this that a more liberal entry condition, which classified 'I' along with (say) 'Hesperus', would *not* be epistemological. For while there are some facts about the sense of 'I' – facts about the verification of first-person sentences, say, or about the way an understanding of 'I' is acquired – which Anscombe's 'logician' is not interested in, it would be a mistake to say that the facts he *is* interested in are facts about its logical syntax *rather than* its sense. For among the things one must know about the name 'Hesperus' in order to be able to use it correctly are that it *is* a name, that it figures in inferences in certain ways, may be substituted in certain contexts *salva veritate* for other names: in short, that it has a certain logical syntax. So, if the sense of an expression is what one needs to know in order to be able to use it correctly, an expression's logical syntax is *a feature of* its sense. Hence if expressions divide into semantic categories according to the kinds of knowledge required for their correct use – and so if the semantic category of referring expression is rightly viewed as an epistemological one – there remains every reason to think that a classification of expressions based on their common logical syntax will be significant.

To concede that 'I' is a referring expression would be to concede that, to put it Wittgensteinianly, the grammar of 'I' and the grammar of 'Hesperus' 'run for a stretch over parallel tracks',[32] and that this

[30] Ibid., p. 534.

[31] Compare Wittgenstein's claim that the function/argument analysis of the predicate calculus is a 'projection of countless different logical forms' (L. Wittgenstein, *Philosophical Grammar*, ed. Rush Rhees, trans Anthony Kenny [Oxford: Blackwell, 1974], p. 205). It is one thing, however, to say that function/argument analysis does not reveal every difference of logical form which there is to be revealed, and another to say that it classifies expressions in an arbitrary manner, or points to similarities in form where there are none.

[32] The phrase is from G. P. Baker and P. M. S. Hacker, *Wittgenstein: Meaning and Understanding, Essays on the Philosophical Investigations*, vol. I (Oxford: Blackwell, 1980), p. 346, acknowledging Wittgenstein, *Philosophical Investigations*, trans G. E. M. Anscombe (Oxford: Blackwell, 1978), p. 192.

common grammar is a sufficiently fundamental feature of both expressions to warrant the conclusion that if 'Hesperus' is a referring expression then 'I' is. It is not to deny, however, that there may not also be extremely important differences between the members of that category in respect of the kinds of sense they have: indeed just because the entry condition for the category is so basic, a multiplicity of higher-level differences is only to be expected. Though 'The First Person' is most often identified with the no reference thesis, much of its importance lies in its attempt to understand the respects in which the sense of 'I' differs, perhaps uniquely, from the kinds of sense possessed by other members of the category of referring expressions, and it is to this aspect of Anscombe's paper that I now turn.

5 In search of higher-level differences in sense between 'I' and other members of the category of referring expressions, I want to return to Anscombe's idea that 'I' is not associated with any conception of an object in the sense explained above, or, in another of Anscombe's formulations, that 'there is no path from 'I' to the person whereby he connects it with an object (the person that he is)'.[33] I shall call this henceforth the 'no conception' thesis.

Anscombe argues for the no reference thesis on the grounds that any attempt to specify a conception through which the referent of the putative referring expression 'I' is 'reached' by one who uses it leads to absurdity, together with the claim that an expression is a referring expression only if it is associated with a conception of an object. But, as I have argued, the conclusion of this *reductio* argument is false. Does this show that the no conception thesis is false as well?

Surely not. If the no reference thesis is taken modestly, as based on a non-standard definition of 'referring expression', the objection to it depends on an objection not to the no conception thesis *per se*, but only to the idea that a relatively high-level epistemological feature such as association with a conception should be favoured over logical syntax as the test for referring expressionhood. If on the other hand the no reference thesis is taken strongly, as having consequences for the logical form of first person sentences, then the proper conclusion from its falsity is not that the no conception thesis is false, but that we have no right to identify the property of being associated with a conception of an object, or of expressing 'what Frege called an "Art des Gegebenseins"', with the property of having the kind of sense characteristic of a Fregean *Eigenname*.[34] On the contrary, it must at least be possible for an expression, thanks to

[33] See Anscombe, 'The Subjectivity of Sensation', p. 55.
[34] See above, section 2, p. 31.

its logical syntax alone, to have the kind of sense which is characteristic of all Fregean *Eigennamen* simply as such, and yet not to be associated with any conception of an object at all.

However, though we do not yet have any reason to reject the no conception thesis, we do not yet have any reason to accept it either. But if it could be shown that the *only* thing wrong with Anscombe's *reductio* argument for the no reference thesis is its reliance on the claim – let us call it [R] – that an expression is a referring expression only if it is associated with a conception of an object, this would prove it to be a good argument for the no conception thesis.

To try to show this, I shall consider a rather skeletal version of Anscombe's *reductio* argument for the no reference thesis, in which [R] does not figure explicitly. It goes as follows. If 'I' is a referring expression, then its referent must be 'really present' to consciousness whenever 'I' is comprehendingly used.[35] Because I can still make comprehending use of 'I' when in a state of 'sensory deprivation', its referent must be something which would continue to be 'really present' to consciousness in such circumstances.[36] But only a Cartesian Ego would satisfy that requirement,[37] and the notion of a Cartesian Ego is incoherent.[38] So "I" is not a referring expression.

Following Andrew Hamilton,[39] I shall refer to this argument as 'the Real Presence argument'. Hamilton contends that the argument fails to establish its intended conclusion. Now it is no part of my purpose to rehabilitate the no reference thesis, or to argue for [R]. But I shall argue, against Hamilton, that if [R] is granted, the Real Presence argument is valid; and if I am right about that, then the 'no conception' thesis is true.

6 Before I turn to Hamilton's attack, two preliminary remarks are needed. First, I am going to assume that Anscombe's strictures against Descartes's notion of a thinking thing are in order, or, if they are not, that other arguments can be found which do the same work. Secondly, a word on 'real presence'. Anscombe says that the referent

[35] 'The First Person', p. 28.

[36] Anscombe, *Collected Philosophical Papers*, vol. II, p. 31.

[37] Ibid.: 'Nothing but a Cartesian Ego will serve'.

[38] Descartes's position has, for example, 'the intolerable difficulty of requiring an identification of the same referent in different "I"-thoughts' (ibid.); and in any case, how 'could one justify the assumption that there is just one thinking which is this thinking of this thought that I am thinking, just one thinker? How do I know that "I" is not ten thinkers thinking in unison?' (ibid.).

[39] Andrew Hamilton, 'Anscombian and Cartesian Scepticism', *Philosophical Quarterly* 41, 162 (1991), pp. 39–54. Hamilton sets the argument out in far more detail than I have.

The first person: problems of sense and reference

of 'I' must be 'present to consciousness' whenever 'I' is comprehendingly used, and then adds that '"presence to consciousness" here
means physical or real presence, not just that one is thinking of the
thing'.[40] The idea is that the referent of 'I' must be present to one's
consciousness in the way that a ballpoint pen is present to one's consciousness when one is looking at it and holding it in one's hand. This
seems to assume a perceptual or quasi-perceptual model of self-
knowledge, in particular of knowledge of one's thoughts, and such a
model may well be wrong. But let us follow Anscombe in granting
this assumption to her Cartesian opponent, since neither Hamilton's
criticisms nor my reply to it do anything with the assumption.

Hamilton dismisses the 'Real Presence' argument on the grounds
that it is false that if 'I' is a referring expression, its referent must be
'really present' to consciousness. Let us call this the real presence
premise. He gives two reasons why he thinks Anscombe maintains
the premise, first that 'if the thinking did not guarantee the presence, the existence of the referent could be doubted', and secondly
that 'real presence is required to ensure that there is no unnoticed
substitution of "I"; that I correctly re-identify the same self'. To
the first reason, Hamilton replies that:

> the thinking itself guarantees the existence, simply as a conse-
> quence of what has been termed the self-reference principle (that
> it is she herself the thinker is thinking about).

And to the second, he replies (citing Evans) that if the *same* subject
has different thoughts at different times, then it goes without saying
that 'I', in each successive thought, will refer to the same thing
(supposing that it refers at all). But that the subject *is* the same both
times is simply a feature of the way Anscombe describes the case, so
the apparent 'logical guarantee' against unnoticed substitution
requires no deeper explanation than that.[41]

Before I reply to these points, I want to set out what I take to be
Anscombe's argument for the real presence premise. Anscombe
asserts the real presence premise having dismissed the idea that "I"
is either an ordinary proper name or a disguised definite description, making the assumption that since it is neither of these, if it is
a referring expression at all, it must be a demonstrative ('There is no
other pronoun but a demonstrative to which "I" could plausibly be
assimilated as a singular term that provides a reference'[42]). Let us go
along with this assumption for the time being.

[40] 'The First Person', p. 28.
[41] All quotations in this paragraph are from Hamilton, 'Anscombian and
Cartesian Scepticism', (*Philosophical Quarterly* 41, 1991), p. 42.
[42] 'The First Person', p. 28.

Now demonstratives, according to Anscombe, require something to 'latch on to' if they are to be correctly used, that is, something – an object, perhaps, or an appearance – with which the user of the demonstrative is presented.[43] Even so, a demonstrative can fail of reference if the object it 'latches on to' does not coincide with its intended referent. Thus in Anscombe's example of 'that is all that is left of poor Jones',[44] the demonstrative latches on to a visually presented box, but its intended referent – whose nature is specified by the answer to 'that what?' – is a parcel of ashes, and the box is empty.

If we continue to suppose that if 'I' is a referring expression at all it must be a demonstrative, the above view of demonstratives implies that whenever 'I' is correctly used there must be something for it to latch on to; that is, there must be *something* which is 'really present' to the user of 'I' every time 'I' is correctly used. Now it is ordinarily possible to refer demonstratively to, say, a human being when that with which one is perceptually presented, and which one's demonstrative therefore perforce latches on to, is no more than a pair of boots glimpsed from one's vantage-point underneath the piano. But in a case of this sort, the boots might turn out to be unoccupied, so one's demonstrative would fail of reference. But this does not seem possible with 'I': if 'I' is a referring expression at all, it is a referring expression secure against reference-failure. So, again on the supposition that 'I' is a referring expression only if it is a demonstrative, the only way for it to be secure against reference-failure is if the object it latches on to and its intended referent cannot fail to coincide. It follows that, since what 'I' latches on to must be 'really present' to consciousness, its intended referent must be 'really present' to consciousness too. This is the "real presence" premise.

The rest of Anscombe's *reductio* then follows smoothly. 'I' may be correctly used in a state of sensory deprivation, so what it latches on to must be something which remains 'really present' to the user even in those circumstances, and only *thinking* – the thinking that is called into existence by the thinking of a first person thought – fulfils that requirement.[45]

[43] Ibid.
[44] Ibid.
[45] It should now be clear why the assumption of a perceptual or quasi-perceptual model of knowledge that one is thinking is harmless for the sake of the argument. For to refuse to grant this assumption and maintain that, in a state of sensory deprivation, one is not in any sort of perceptual (or quasi-perceptual) contact with the thing one is would be to go a long way at a very early stage to conceding that 'I' cannot be a demonstrative.

But the fact that the intended referent of 'I' cannot fail to be identical with what 'I' latches on to sets strict limits to the nature of the conception which may be associated with it, and here this means that the associated conception must be such that – unlike the pair of boots and 'this human being' – the item which 'I' latches on to manifestly fits it. So the associated conception must be 'thinking' ('what conception can be suggested, other than that of *thinking*, the thinking of the I-thought, which secures this guarantee against reference-failure?'[46]). So if 'I' is a referring expression at all, it refers to *this thinking thing*.[47]

7 The truth of the real presence premise is confirmed, then, if two assumptions are granted: first, that if 'I' is a referring expression it must be a demonstrative and, secondly, Anscombe's view of demonstratives.

I offered a brief defence of Anscombe's view of demonstratives in section 1. Anscombe's first assumption, however, is more controversial. It rests, in the first place, on her claim that 'I' is neither a proper name nor a disguised definite description. There is no problem with these negative claims in themselves.[48] But unless proper name, demonstrative and (perhaps) definite description are the *only* categories of referring expression, these negative claims do not establish Anscombe's first assumption. What the three categories have in common is that every member of each is associated with a conception by way of which it attaches to its referent. But even supposing that the categories of referring expression associated with a conception are limited to these three, Anscombe's first assumption is not acceptable unless an expression is a referring expression only if it attaches to an object by way of a conception, that is, unless [R] is true.

Now if [R] is true, it will not be possible to appeal, as Hamilton does in his first criticism of the Real Presence argument, to what he

[46] 'The First Person', p. 29.

[47] Taking the word 'thing' here to imply temporally extended existence would be optimistic: the considerations which show that if 'I' refers demonstratively by way of a conception, then it refers to a thing whose essence is thinking may also show that if it refers demonstratively by way of a conception, then it refers to a momentary existent.

[48] The argument against the claim that 'I' is a proper name is that, if it were, one could make a false first person judgment having misidentified an object as the referent of 'I', and one cannot. For arguments against the view that 'I' is a disguised definite description, see e.g. John Perry, 'Frege on Demonstratives', in Perry, *The Problem of the Essential Indexical and Other Essays* (New York and Oxford: Oxford University Press, 1993), pp. 3–25.

Edward Harcourt

calls the 'self-reference principle' since, by [R], an expression may be governed by that principle and yet fail to qualify as a referring expression. A similar point applies to Hamilton's second criticism. If 'I' is governed by the 'self-reference principle', then sameness of reference of 'I' on two distinct occasions of use is indeed guaranteed merely by the stipulation that the user is, on each occasion, the same. If, however, 'I' were a demonstrative (or indeed a proper name), sameness of reference secured in this way would not be enough for the user, having used it once, to re-use it on a second occasion with any confidence: for that, the user would need not only to pick out what is *in fact* the same referent on both occasions, but to re-identify the referent picked out on the second occasion as the one picked out on the first. So, given that the referent of 'I' would have to be 'really present' to the I-user on its first occasion of use, knowledge that the referent is the same on the second occasion requires, as Anscombe says, that it also 'remain in view so long as something was being taken to be *I*',[49] and this is not guaranteed merely by the 'self-reference principle'. It turns out, then, that *if* we accept [R], the Real Presence argument succeeds.

As we have seen, however, we should not accept [R],[50] so Hamilton is right that the Real Presence argument fails to establish the no reference thesis. But it emerges also that *all* that is wrong with the Real Presence argument is its reliance on [R], and from this it follows in turn that the Real Presence argument is a successful argument for the no conception thesis. Though less radical than the no reference thesis, this is a valuable conclusion about the kind of understanding we have of 'I'. For very many referring expressions *are* associated with conceptions in this way. So in not being associated with a conception in the way 'Paris' or 'that dog' is, 'I' is a referring expression of an exceptional kind.

8 We began by asking whether the logical and epistemological peculiarities of 'I' – its irreducibility, its apparent guarantee against reference-failure, the immunity to error through misidentification of (some if not all) first person judgments – might be explained, in Fregean fashion, by appeal to the mode of presentation which 'I' expresses, or to the conception by way of which 'I' 'reaches' its referent. We have seen that, *pace* Anscombe, we must allow that, at a very basic level, the correct account of 'I' coincides with the account which the Fregean would give, in that 'I' has the kind of sense characteristic of a referring expression simply as such. Once shorn of [R], however, Anscombe's *reductio* argument shows that

[49] 'The First Person', pp. 30–1.
[50] See above, section 4.

44

taking the Fregean account any further puts a common-sense view of the kind of thing 'I' stands for out of reach. The force of Anscombe's argument is thus to show that one cannot both have a full-dress Fregean account of the relation between 'I' and the thing it stands for and hold that 'I' stands for the human being who utters it. None the less the explanation Anscombe envisages of the peculiarities of 'I' appeals to the kind of understanding we have of it, and is thus of the same general type as the Fregean's. The no reference thesis apart, what makes room on Anscombe's account for the fact that 'I' refers to the same thing as some non-first-personal designation of the human being who utters it is not the special character of the conception by way of which 'I' attaches to its referent but another fact about our understanding of it, the very fact that it does *not* attach to its referent by way of a conception.[51] Indeed Frege's inability to say anything more about the mode of presentation associated with 'I' than that it is 'special and primitive' may perhaps be seen, retrospectively, as an oblique expression of discomfort with the idea that it is associated with a mode of presentation at all.[52]

References

Altham, J. E. J., 'Indirect Reflexives and Indirect Speech', in Cora Diamond and Jenny Teichman (eds), *Intention and Intentionality: Essays in Honour of G. E. M. Anscombe* (Brighton: Harvester Press, 1979), pp. 25–38.

Anscombe, G. E. M., 'The First Person', in Anscombe, *Collected Philosophical Papers, vol. II: Metaphysics and the Philosophy of Mind* (Oxford: Blackwell, 1981), pp. 21–36.

——, 'The Subjectivity of Sensation', in Anscombe, *Collected Philosophical Papers, vol. II: Metaphysics and the Philosophy of Mind* (Oxford: Blackwell, 1981), pp. 44–56.

Baker, G. P. and Hacker, P. M. S., *Meaning and Understanding: Essays on the Philosophical Investigations, vol. I* (Oxford: Blackwell, 1980).

Castañeda, H.-N., '"He": A Study in the Logic of Self-Consciousness', *Ratio,* 8 (1966), pp. 130–57.

Dummett, Michael, *Frege: Philosophy of Language* (2nd edition, London: Duckworth, 1981).

Evans, Gareth, *The Varieties of Reference* (Oxford: Clarendon Press, 1982).

[51] 'The First Person' also has much to say by way of a characterisation of a speaker's understanding of 'I', taking off from the idea that the first person distinctively expresses one's knowledge without observation of the thing one is. But I cannot explore that aspect of Anscombe's paper here.

[52] Here I ignore complications to do with the distinction between the 'I' of soliloquy and the 'I' of communication.

Edward Harcourt

Geach, P. T., 'On Beliefs about Oneself', in Geach, *Logic Matters* (Oxford: Blackwell, 1972), pp. 128–9.

——, review of Evans, *The Varieties of Reference*, *Philosophy*, 61 (Oct. 1986), pp. 534–40.

Hacker, P. M. S., *Wittgenstein: Meaning and Mind, An Analytical Commentary on the Philosophical Investigations, vol. III* (Oxford: Blackwell, 1990).

Hamilton, Andrew, 'Anscombian and Cartesian Scepticism', *Philosophical Quarterly*, 41, (162) (1991), pp. 39–54.

James, William, *The Principles of Psychology* (2 vols, London: Macmillan, 1891).

Moore, G. E., 'Wittgenstein's Lectures in 1930–33', *Mind*, 64 (1955), pp. 1–27.

Perry, John, 'Frege on Demonstratives', in Perry, *The Problem of the Essential Indexical and Other Essays* (New York and Oxford: Oxford University Press, 1993), pp. 3–25.

Wiggins, David, *Sameness and Substance* (Oxford: Blackwell, 1980).

Williams, C. J. F., 'Myself', *Ratio* (New Series) 4 (1991).

Wittgenstein, Ludwig, *On Certainty*, eds. G. E. M. Anscombe and G. H. von Wright, trans D. Paul and G. E. M. Anscombe (Oxford: Blackwell, 1979).

——, *Philosophical Grammar*, ed. Rush Rhees, trans Anthony Kenny (Oxford: Blackwell, 1974).

——, *Philosophical Investigations*, trans G. E. M. Anscombe (Oxford: Blackwell, 1978).

——, *The Blue and Brown Books* (Oxford: Blackwell, 1978).

Wright, Crispin, *Frege's Conception of Numbers as Objects* (Aberdeen University Press, 1983).

An empiricist defence of singular causes

NANCY CARTWRIGHT

1 Methodological empiricism and what it teaches about causation

Empiricism has traditionally been concerned with two questions:
(a) What is the source of our concepts and ideas? and (b) How
should claims to empirical knowledge be judged? The empiricist
answer to the first question is 'From observation or experience.'
The concern in the second question is not to ground science in pure
observation or in direct experience, but rather to ensure that claims
to scientific knowledge are judged against the natural phenomena
themselves. Questions about nature must be settled by nature – not
by faith, nor metaphysics, nor mathematics, and not by convention
or convenience either. From Francis Bacon to Karl Popper empiricists have wanted to police the methods of scientific enquiry.

I am going to talk here about empiricism and causation. But I
shall address only one of the empiricist's two concerns. I shall not
ask where our concept of causation comes from or what it corresponds to; instead I will look to see what kinds of causal claims can
be established and by what methods. The outcome is unfavourable
for those empiricists, who, following Hume, spurn singular causes.
For the Humean, a singular causal claim cannot be established
directly; we first need a general claim, based on a regular association. Professor Anscombe maintains just the opposite.[1] For her, singular causes are primary. There may well be a regularity corresponding to each singular fact, but the regularity does not constitute
the truth of the singular claim, nor is it necessary for its confirmation. We can, after all, *see* that the cat is lapping up the milk.

Admittedly most causal facts of interest to contemporary science
cannot just be seen to be true. The example I shall discuss in section 3 is typical – the iron bar in the Einstein–de Haas experiment
gyrated just so *because of* the rotation induced in the electrons by the
oscillating magnetic field. More sophisticated methods than bare
observation are necessary here. Some of these methods follow the
Humean programme and aim to establish regularities; for example,

---

[1] See especially Anscombe's, 'Causality and Determination: An
Inaugural Lecture' (London: Cambridge University Press, 1971).

the stratified sampling techniques of sociology or the controlled experiments of the medical sciences. But others, like the 'one-shot' experiments of physics, test singular claims directly. I am going to argue that Anscombe is right. Regularities have no privileged position. Singular claims can be established just as reliably.

The argument depends on a careful look at what a regularity view prescribes: exactly what kind of regularities must be established to test a causal claim? One-shot experiments work in disciplines like physics that can supply a large amount of background information, enough to guarantee that the experiment isolates the one sequence of events in question. The logic of these experiments involves a complex network of deductions from premises antecedently accepted, and a good number of these premises are themselves causal.

It is not surprising from the Humean point of view that singular confirmation of this kind is possible once one is operating within such a set of assumptions. What is surprising, I think, is that no causal conclusions are possible outside such assumptions. Without antecedent information it is no more possible to establish a causal claim via a regularity than it is to demonstrate a singular cause directly – and in both cases the causal inputs must include not only general causal laws but singular facts as well. Contrary to the conventional views inspired by Hume, the empiricist demand for testability does not favour regularities over singular causes.

This conclusion nicely brings together the doctrines of philosophic empiricism with the more practical empiricism of working science. In raising the second of the two empiricist questions I am invoking a philosophic tradition concerned with the methods and rules of scientific judgment. The tradition begins in the scientific revolution with philosophers like Bacon, Gassendi, and Boyle, and later includes Whewell, Mill, Mach, Bridgman, and other familiar figures. The philosophic tradition runs parallel to a scientific one that can be seen in specific empiricist practices in different sciences at different periods. In this practical empiricist tradition, singular causes are no problem. They are treated, for instance, by the one-shot experiments of contemporary physics, which I have already mentioned. An example of a very different sort can be found in the work of Claud Bernard, an important late nineteenth-century French clinician and diagnostician. Bernard's clinical methods were explicitly based on his rejection of statistical reasoning and his insistence that only detailed studies of the single case can provide sure evidence about the causes of disease. In general I think it should be unsettling when the philosophical doctrines of empiricism and practical doctrines diverge. Hume's view that we can lay our philosophy aside when we leave the study and enter the laboratory is ultimately unsatisfactory. It is thus an important side-benefit of Anscombe's position, and the arguments for it given here, that empiricist philosophy and empiricist practice are brought together.

The empiricist tradition I describe is often associated with other views that serve different purposes. Two, which are fairly widely discredited now, are the verificationist theory of meaning and the foundational picture of knowledge. The verificationist theory requires not only that scientific propositions be tested severally; the tests must double as definitions. But even in the heyday of operationalism, few empiricists really followed Bridgman in joining the jobs of testing and defining.

On the foundational theory of knowledge, the tests, traced backwards, must ultimately be capable of conferring certainty. But it is easy to decouple the requirement that claims be tested from the requirement that the tests supply infallibility. Indeed this is necessary if causal claims are to be tested at all, given the arguments here that any method for establishing a causal claim requires causes antecedently. The two doctrines have different motivations. Foundationalists want to guarantee the possibility of error-free knowledge. They insist that reasons be good enough to ensure certainty, whereas empiricists are concerned with the question of what counts as a good reason at all. Only nature can provide reasons for empirical judgments.

The empiricist doctrine, though weaker than verificationism or foundationalism, is nevertheless a demanding view, and one not universally followed in science, particularly in modern physics. The demand for renormalisable theories in quantum electrodynamics, or the constraints imposed on the range of cosmological models by the desire to eliminate various singularities, are two examples. In both cases it is mathematical considerations that shape the theory and not judgments imposed by the phenomena. Also, as Bas van Fraassen insists, use of the hypothetical–deductive method is ruled out as well. Empiricism would thus have significant consequences if it were generally adopted. But – as I shall argue here – the consequences do not include the elimination of singular causal claims.

So much for the second of the two empiricist concerns that I described at the start. What of the first? Is there a reasonable source in experience for our concept of single case causation? Again, Professor Anscombe thinks there is. But this is not an issue I will discuss here, except to hope that she is right. Otherwise the empiricist position is split, one concern admitting singular causes, the other ruling them out. If this should happen, I would urge in favour of singular causes, since concerns about admissibility are closer to real scientific problems than are worries about the sources of ideas;

and where philosophy comes close to practice it is bound to be better. The effectiveness of different views serves as a check on our abstract philosophical defences of them.

2 Regularity methods and the need for singular causes

Since the end of the nineteenth century it has been clear that a regularity account must give up universal association and look instead for some kind of probabilistic connection if it is to provide a genuine method for testing and establishing causal claims. In this section I am going to look to see what follows when we make explicit exactly what this probabilistic connection is.

The best probabilistic accounts take positive correlation as their leading idea: causes may not be constantly conjoined with their effects, as Hume supposed, but at least they should increase their frequency. Formally $P(E/C) > P(E/-C)$. But correlations can be misleading. The most well-known case is the problem of spurious correlations, sometimes also called the problem of joint effects: A may be correlated with B not because A causes B or *vice versa*, but because they are both effects of the joint cause C.

This is a special case of a more general problem that I have discussed before.[2] Here A and B are correlated with each other because they are both correlated with a third factor, the joint cause C. But the third factor need not be a cause of A and B; nor must the correlation of A or B with the third factor be positive. Any correlation with any other causal factors can render misleading correlations – or the lack of them – between A and B. This is because of a rather surprising statistical fact called Simpson's paradox: any fact about correlations in a population can be reversed by partitioning into subpopulations. Or conversely any fact true in the subpopulations can be reversed by averaging to the whole population. A and B may for instance have positive – or zero – correlation in the population, and yet be negatively correlated in both subpopulations.

Here is an example. Imagine smoking (S) causes heart disease (H). But smoking is highly correlated with an even stronger preventative, say exercise (X). Then smoking may in fact decrease the probability of heart disease in the population, even though it increases the probability both in the subpopulation of exercisers

[2] N. Cartwright, *How the Laws of Physics Lie* (Oxford University Press, 1983).

and in the non-exercisers. Since smokers are (we are supposing) very likely to be exercisers, if the beneficial effects of the exercising dominate the harmful effects of smoking, the incidence of heart disease among smokers will be less than in the total population.

Here is one more example to show how Simpson's paradox operates. The graduate school at Berkeley was accused of discriminating against women: averaging across all departments the acceptance rate for women was considerably lower than that for men. But the university was exonerated from the charge, for when stratified by department, this is no longer the case. Department by department, women were doing as well or better than the men. Why then was the *average* acceptance rate for women lower? Because women were applying to the harder departments. That is, women tended to apply to departments with high rejection rates. Being a woman did not cause rejection; it only looked that way because being a woman was correlated with a different, more legitimate reason for rejection.

The solution to Simpson's paradox is to test for correlations between A and B in very special populations – those for which all other causal factors relevant to B are held fixed. In such a population, there *can* be no background correlations between C and any other causal factor to generate misleading connections between A and B. So we look not at $P(E/C)$ and $P(E/-C)$ but rather at $P(E/C \pm F_1 \ldots \pm F_n)$ versus $P(E/-C \pm F_1 \ldots \pm F_n)$, for each of the possible arrangements of other causal factors, $F_1, \ldots, F_n$. The conditional probability that we see here, for E given C, holding fixed other factors, is called the *partial conditional probability*. It is closely connected with the technique of *stratification* commonly used in the social sciences to separate out the effects of confounding variables. For instance, in looking for the effect of education on later earning power, one uses other possibly relevant variables – family income, father's education, race, etc. – to stratify the population into layers. Then one looks within each layer for a correlation between education and earning power.

Very roughly then we arrive at the following condition for establishing the claim that C *causes* E.[3]

$$CC: P(E/C \pm F_1 \pm \ldots \pm F_n) > P(E/-C \pm F_1 \pm \ldots \pm F_n)$$

I call each of the homogeneous subpopulations in which there is a fixed arrangement of the F_i, *test* populations for C causes E. The list of factors $F_1, \ldots, F_n$ is supposed to include all the other factors causally relevant to E. So here causality intrudes into what was meant to be a pure regularity account. We set out to write down

[3] This formulation is from Cartwright, *How the Laws of Physics Lie*. CC^* is a new formulation.

what probabilistic association must obtain in order to support the claim that C causes E. But in order to know what particular probabilistic association to look for, we must presuppose a good deal of antecedent causal knowledge – we must know all the other kinds of factors that could bring about the effect besides the one in question.

The formula is, as I said, rough. There are a large number of caveats and details to be filled in. There is one detail that I want to concentrate on, for it is central to my claim about singular causes. The point seems almost trivial at first, but turns out to be of considerable consequence. Formula CC says that for the claim C *causes* E to hold, C must increase the probability of E in every test population. But this condition is too strong, for it holds fixed too much; we should hold fixed other causally relevant features only in individuals in whom these features are not the effects of C itself.

The simplest case has this structure:

Imagine a genuine cause C, which operates through K. K can, however, occur on its own, in which case it is still positively effective for E. If we hold K fixed, we erroneously infer that C does not cause E, for $P(E/C \pm K) = P(E/-C \pm K)$. This is a familiar point: intermediate effects in a process (here K) screen off the initial cause (C) from the final outcome (E). If we hold K fixed in this kind of case, we may fail to identify genuine causes when we have them.

Elliott Sober and Ellery Eells have given an everyday illustration of this structure. Imagine you dial my number on the phone, my telephone rings and I lift the receiver. Your dialling caused me to do so. Concomitantly, it seems true to say that your dialling increased the probability of my lifting the receiver. But now, hold fixed the intermediate event of my phone ringing. *Given* that my phone rings, surely we do not expect that, 'I am more likely to lift the receiver if it is you who calls than I am if it isn't.'[4] Because the ringing is in this case an event itself caused by your dialling and because it is not an independent occurrence which may have its own separate influence on my behaviour, it must be treated differently from the factors that make trouble in Simpson's paradox. The individual causal histories matter.

We need then to add something like the following restriction to get the characterisation of test populations right.

[4] Ellery, Eells and Elliott Sober, 'Probabilistic Causality and the Question of Transitivity', *Philosophy of Science*, 50 (1983), p. 40.

52

An empiricist defence of singular causes

CC^*: Test populations must be homogeneous with respect to other causal factors except for those individual cases where the presence or absence of the factor is brought about by C itself. These individuals belong in the test population where they would otherwise have been were it not for the action of C.

Call the amended version of CC with this restriction added, CC^*.

Empiricists certainly will not like this restriction, which mentions not only singular causal histories, but even counterfactual singular causal histories. Perhaps the use of counterfactuals can be avoided. But I think the reference to singular causes cannot. There are at least two good proposals that I know for doing so, and neither of them work. But the discussion becomes quite technical and complicated, so I will not go into the details. I will briefly describe a third strategy because it is of such practical importance – the controlled experiment.

The point of 'control' in controlled experiment is to eliminate the confounding effects of other causal variables without requiring that we know specifically which these variables are. This connects immediately with our discussion of Simpson's paradox. If we tried to apply formula CC^* directly to a test causal claim, we would usually not get very far. CC^* instructs us to look for an increased frequency of Es among Cs in populations homogeneous with respect to all other relevant factors. In most cases we have no idea what most of these other factors are. The controlled experiment gives a way around the problem. Random sampling is supposed to ensure that the unknown variables have the same distribution in the control group as in the test group, and this has two critical advantages. First, the effects of these variables will be the same in both groups so that any difference between the two must be due to the putative cause; second, there will be no correlations between any of these variables and the putative cause that could generate a Simpson's paradox. *Prima facie* the controlled experiment eliminates the need for antecedent causal information which is so damaging to the Hume programme.

In fact it does not do so. It minimises the need for background causal information but does not eliminate it. We must still use causal language, I believe, to characterise what a controlled experiment is. Far worse, because it undermines the practical utility of a tool which is widespread and hard to replace, the controlled experiment is not reliable. Unlike the problems with Simpson's paradox, controlled experiments cannot solve the kind of problem which leads to the introduction of singular causal histories.[5] As a consequence

---

[5] For a discussion of this problem, see N. Cartwright, 'What's wrong with controlled experiments?', manuscript, (Stanford University, 1985).

there are a wide range of cases for which even an ideal controlled experiment will give wrong results. Since there is no general way to tell which these cases are, the problem is serious, for the controlled experiment is widely acknowledged to be the most reliable method for testing hypotheses in the social and medical sciences.

It is important to be clear exactly what kind of reliability is at stake here. There are various sources of uncertainty in testing a hypothesis. I take it that the only good methods are ones in which all the uncertainty has an epistemic origin; it arises entirely from the unavoidable possibility that we may be mistaken about things we take to be true, and not from any structural inability in the method itself. Any method requires its own special kinds of background assumptions, about which we may of course be mistaken. We assume, for example, that the machine is operating as we expect, that our samples are representative, that our calibrations are based on appropriate corrections, and so forth. But we may ask, 'How sure is the output *given* the input?' In a reliable method, as I use the term here, the verdict will be exactly as certain as our background assumptions. There is no inherent slippage between the method and what it is supposed to establish. The method, correctly applied, will give an answer one way or the other.

This is exactly what the controlled experiment cannot do. Even in the most ideal case where all the background assumptions are met – the experimental populations are indeed representative, the putative cause alone distinguishes the two groups at the start, and so forth – there is no univocal way to read the results. The hypothesis is not genuinely tested by the experiment. This contrasts with how CC^* is supposed to work. The method of complete stratification is difficult to apply, but when correctly applied, it gives a reliable answer.

We can now see the relevance of this contrast to the Hume program. Controlled experiments fail, leaving CC^* as the only reliable method for establishing causal hypotheses via regularities, and CC^* requires both generic and singular causal information as input. But once we allow this kind of input singular causal claims can be established by methods just as reliable.[6] I turn to these methods in the next section.

3 Direct methods to study single causes

I take as a model for establishing singular causal claims the so-called 'one-shot' experiments of physics. Here statistics play no role. We

[6] In fact, I do not think CC^* works as well as I say here, for it cannot handle cases where the same factor can both cause and prevent a given result along different paths. For a discussion of this point, see N. Cartwright, 'Reply to Eells and Dupré', manuscript, (Stanford University, 1985).

do not repeat the experiment a large number of times and look to see what kind of association results. In principle a single run suffices.[7] I have said that no method will give accurate causal knowledge out without putting causal knowledge in. Like $CC*$, one-shot experiments assume a good deal of background knowledge, and that in part is how they can function as reliable indicators. They require both a vast amount of causal information and a considerable ability to control the environment. The knowledge in fact must be so complete that we know, when the effect occurs, that only the putative cause could have brought it about; it could have arisen in no other way, given that the apparatus functioned according to plan.

This kind of completeness is notoriously difficult to achieve. But in physics we are aided by a number of factors: (1) We already know a lot about what other factors could and could **not bring** about the effect. This is in no way certain knowledge, but it is knowledge about which we sometimes have practical certainty – we know it well enough. (2) The exact effect we are looking for can be specified very precisely, so that the range of alternative causes for just that effect is drastically confined. In the example I shall describe – some experiments by Einstein and de Haas – they were looking not just for an induced rotation, but for a rotation *of a very specific size*. (3) In physics we have impressive practical skills, both at building and at measuring what we want. The measuring is important because it ensures that we can fill in some of the parameters in the background conditions by empirical test and not by theoretical calculation. This is one of the ways in which the Einstein–de Haas experiments went wrong – they calculated rather than measured a number of factors, such as the saturation magnetisation and the field of their solenoid.

The Einstein–de Haas experiments are an instructive example, providing a case where the method misfired, so that it is easy in retrospect to see what further information was needed for an assur-

---

[7] Of course not all experiments in physics are one-shot. See Peter Galison's *How Experiments End* (University of Chicago Press), especially chapter 10, for an extended discussion of some experiments in physics where statistics matter. But even in those experiments the point of statistics is not to establish a regular association and thereby a causal connection, but instead to provide evidence that makes it improbable that the data could have a different cause than the one hypothesised. One-shot experiments are often repeated as well. But again the repetition serves other purposes – for example to ensure that the machine is operating properly – and does not aim to establish a statistical regularity. Cf. Allan Franklin and Colin Howson, 'Why do Scientists Prefer to Vary their Experiments?' *Studies in History and Philosophy of Science*, 15 (1984), pp. 51– 62.

Nancy Cartwright

ance that the test would work. In 1914 Einstein and W. J. de Haas set out to test the hypothesis: magnetism is caused by orbiting electrons. They tested it by suspending an iron bar in an oscillating magnetic field and measuring the gyrations induced when the bar was magnetised. You expect the bar to oscillate when the field is turned on and off because electrons have mass and when they start to rotate they will produce an angular momentum. The ratio of this momentum to the magnetic moment – called the gyromagnetic ratio – should be $2m/e$, where m and e are the mass and charge of the electron respectively. This is very close to the answer Einstein and de Haas found. But it is not the result they should have got. Later experiments finally settled on a gyromagnetic ratio about half that size, and nowadays – following the Dirac theory – we attribute the results not to the orbiting electrons but to a complex interaction of orbit and spin-orbit effects. What went wrong with the Einstein–de Haas experiment?

The answer is – a large number of things. I take this example from a paper of Peter Galison's in *Historical Studies in the Physical Sciences*, 1982,[8] and the reader can see the complete details laid out there. Galison describes the work of ten different experimental groups producing dozens of different experimental constructions over a period of ten years to establish finally that the Einstein–de Haas hypothesis was mistaken. I will briefly discuss just one of the factors Galison describes.

Besides the effects of the hypothesised electron motion, it was clear that the magnetic field of the earth itself can also cause a rotation in the bar, so there had to be a shield against this field. 'At first [Einstein and de Haas] used hoops with a radius of one meter with coils wound around them to eliminate the earth's field.'[9] In the next set of experiments de Haas wrapped the wire of the solenoid as well. He also arranged a compensating magnet near the centre of the bar, and two near the poles as well as a neutralising coil at right angles to the bar. In 1915 Samuel Barnett from Ohio State University performed similar experiments, with a great number of improvements. In particular, he neutralised the earth's field with several large coils. As Galison reports, 'the outcome after his exhaustive preparations was a value [of the gyromagnetic ratio] less than half of that expected for orbiting electrons'.[10]

[8] Peter Galison, 'Theoretical Predispositions in Experimental Physics: Einstein and the Gyromagnetic Experiments, 1915–25', *Historical Studies in the Physical Sciences*, 12(2) (1982), pp. 285–323.
[9] Galison, 'Theoretical Predispositions', p. 00.
[10] Galison, 'Theoretical Predispositions', p. 00.

The story goes on, but this is enough to give a sense of the detail of thought and workmanship necessary to get the experiment right. The point is that we sometimes *do* get it right, or, as right as anything else we believe – and more right than most things. We are often apt as philosophers to get lost in grand claims about theory-ladenness, inevitable fallibility, in principle underdetermination, and the like. When we do it is a good idea to stop and to look at some real experiments in physics, to see both how they work, and to see that they do work.

If they did not work, my basic philosophical point here would be moot. I have been trying to distinguish between a kind of epistemic uncertainty that a method can have because of the fallibility of our background knowledge and a more serious in-built uncertainty that arises because the method is not really capable of telling us what we want to know. But if we could never have reasonable confidence in our background assumptions anyway, the distinction would not be worth much.

4 Conclusion

Empiricists have tended to believe that there are no reliable methods for testing singular causal claims directly. But this is a mistake. The one-shot experiments of physics provide an obvious counterinstance. In the one-shot experiment we can bootstrap from knowledge we already have – including singular causal claims about what is going on in the particular apparatus we have designed – to new causal information about the individual objects being experimentally investigated. I use the word 'bootstrap' deliberately, for formally the one-shot experiments can be modelled by Clark Glymour's bootstrap theory of confirmation:[11] The evidence plus the background assumptions deductively imply the hypothesis being tested.

For this to happen the background knowledge must be considerable, essentially enough to rule out any other possible cause. We must be able to construct our apparatus to prevent other causes from operating, or be able to calculate exactly enough how they contribute to the effect, or be sure that we have shielded against them. But the type of causal information required – both singular and general – is no different from what is needed to make reliable regularity-based judgments about causes. Empiricists who hanker for an infallible foundation in the alleged 'raw given' will be frustrated: you cannot get causal knowledge out without putting causal

[11] Clark Glymour, *Theory and Evidence* (Princeton University Press, 1980).

Nancy Cartwright

knowledge in. But then, singular causal claims fare no worse than general ones based on regular associations. This should not be surprising. Physics is commonly agreed to supply our surest scientific knowledge, and physics notoriously does not collect statistics.

Causality and derivativeness

STEPHEN MAKIN

This paper is a reflection on some of Elizabeth Anscombe's influential work on causation, in particular on some comments in her Inaugural Lecture at Cambridge, published as 'Causality and Determination'.[1] One of Anscombe's major concerns in that paper is the relation between causation and necessitation, and she critically discusses the cast of mind which links causality with some kind of necessary connection or with exceptionless generalisation. In place of a semi-technical analysis of causation, Anscombe identifies the obvious and yet little considered core of the causal relation as follows[2]:

> There is something to observe here, that lies under our noses. It is little attended to, yet still so obvious as to seem trite. It is this: causality consists in the derivativeness of an effect from its causes. This is the core, the common feature, of causality in its various kinds. Effects derive from, arise out of, come of, their causes. For example, everyone will grant that physical parenthood is a causal relation. Here the derivation is material, by fission. Now analysis in terms of necessity or universality does not tell us of this derivedness of the effect; rather it forgets about that.

I will consider an account of the causal relation in expansion of this remark of Anscombe's.

I start from the interesting fact that, while contentious philosophical questions about causation abound, we are remarkably successful in managing the concept of a cause before, or while, we are involved with them. For example, some philosophers have thought that causes necessitate their effects, others have denied this. What is remarkable, though, is that philosophers for the most part agree, in any particular case, as to whether this is or is not a causal link. All the work then goes into showing, for example, how (perhaps contrary to appearance) the cause makes the effect necessary, or how this is not so. The concept of a cause seems more perspicuous than many of the notions offered in explication of it: for example, INUS conditions, causal circumstances, the counterfactual dependence of one family of propositions on another. In itself this need not be a

---

[1] All references to this paper are to Anscombe's *Collected Philosophical Papers Volume II: Metaphysics and the Philosophy of Mind* (Oxford: Basil Blackwell, 1981), pp. 133–47.

[2] Ibid., p. 136.

Stephen Makin

point of any great significance: no more significant than the point, for example, that it is easier to pick out reptiles or cases of measles than it is to say what-reptiles-are or what-measles-is. What makes it a significant point, and relevant to what Anscombe says, is that consideration of particular causal set ups, which are *prima facie* problem cases for some views of causation, leads to an interesting account of causation which focuses on the core of causality identified by Anscombe, rather than requiring any prior settling of questions about determinism, indeterminism, counterfactuals, laws of nature and so on. I do not mean to say that such questions should not be discussed: Anscombe herself discusses them, and takes a position on, for example, the issue of whether causes are necessitating. But I do mean to say that if we want to say something enlightening and true about the causal relation, the explanatory notions will not be counterfactual dependence, necessary condition, sufficient condition and so on. The explanatory notion will rather be the derivativeness of an effect from its causes.

Now there is a danger that an account offered of the causal relation in these terms will seem vacuous: and thus Anscombe says that what she has focused on 'is little attended to, and yet still so obvious as to seem trite'.[3] But while the account to be suggested is neutral, in that it does not require prior decision on questions which are apt to divide philosophers in their discussions of causality – and so should be acceptable to all parties – it is not vacuous. It is intended, following Anscombe's lead, to give an account of the core of causality, and to be explanatory of the way in which we pick out causal relations. It does not consist just in saying that it is *plain* that such-and-such *is* while such-and-such *is not* a causal connection. Nor does it simply ignore such notions as necessitation for it gives us terms in which we can say what it is for a cause to be necessitating. Its neutrality lies in its not requiring that we answer the question whether causes as such are necessitating. It might turn out to be true that all causes are necessitating, or that just some are, or perhaps that none are: but we can say what it is for a connection to be causal without deciding that question.

Here is an account of the causal connection, which expands on Anscombe's comment:

> *a*, which is F, causes *b*, which is G, iff there is *a* and there is *b*, and Fs are appropriate to cause, or can cause, Gs.[4]

[3] Ibid., p. 136.

[4] In keeping with the desire to offer something as neutral as possible, I have deliberately stated this account in such a way as to leave open whether we should think of the causal relata *a* and *b* as events (*a*, which is a beheading, causes *b*, which is a death...), in which case *there is a* would be read as *a occurs*, or in some other way (*a*, which is a cream cake, causes *b*, which is obesity...).

This should become clearer and more plausible in the light of examples. But before turning to some examples, I should say something about the locution *appropriate to cause*. When we are considering a purportedly causal set up, there will be certain connections which are possible causal connections, certain connections which are not possible causal connections. In some cases these possibilities will be generated by laws of nature. In other cases talk of 'laws of nature' would not be in place, but there will be comparable explanatory theories (in a loose sense) marking out what are and what are not possible causal routes. In order for this account to be plausible it is not necessary to say anything about laws of nature, other than that they mark out possible causal links. But it is important that the notion of what is appropriate to cause what is not intended simply to shift attention from the causal link on the particular level (*a* causes *b*) to the causal link on the general level (Fs cause Gs). The thought is rather that if there is *a* (which is F) and there is *b* (which is G), and there is a route for getting from *a* to *b* (which will be given by a law of nature linking Fs and Gs), and that route is filled out as required, then there is no more to *a* being the cause of *b*. In particular, it is not necessary to consider what would have happened had there not been *a*; or whether, given that there was *a*, *b* had to follow; or given that there was *a*, the probability of there being *b* increased.

At this point examples are helpful. First, a very favourable example, that of a Galton Board. This example will help to explicate some useful terminology: the idea of a *causal route* and of a causal route's being *filled*. Suppose the board is as shown in Figure 1.

What a route *simpliciter* is in this example is clear enough. It is just a line of pins, viz. a way of getting from one pin to another on the board. A *causal* route is a way of getting from a putative cause to a putative effect. I can illustrate by comparing two routes: ABDG

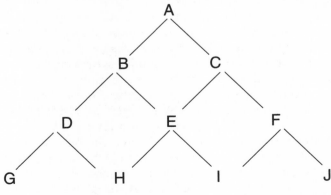

Figure 1.

Stephen Makin

and ABECA. The first gives a causal route, in that any consistently downward movement from pin to pin is allowed by the laws of nature applied to the case. The second route is ruled out as a causal route, since it would require a ball to take an upward path.

Suppose a ball is released at A and then is found at B. Did releasing the ball at A cause it to be present at B? It seems clear to me that it did: for the ball was at A and then was at B, and there is a causal route from A to B: that is, some law gives being-released-at-A as an appropriate cause of being-present-at-B, namely the law of gravity by reference to which it is established that any consistently downward movement from pin to pin is possible.

Now suppose the causal route is more extended: the ball is released at A and then is found at G. We can construct the overall route out of component routes: AB, BD and DG. Again, to say that the release at A causes the presence at G is to say that the ball was released at A, and was present at G, and that there is a causal route from A to G.

But there is a complication. When the route from cause to effect is composed of sub-routes – as it no doubt will be in every case, if space and time are continuous – then it is important to show how the causal connection over the whole route is compounded from causal connections over each sub-route. The release of the ball at A causes its presence at G in that: the release at A causes the presence at B, the release at B causes the presence at D, the release at D causes the presence at G. And that is so in that the ball was at A and then at B, and there is a causal route from A to B; the ball was at B and then at D, and there is a causal route from B to D; the ball was at D and then at G, and there is a causal route from D to G. All this can be abbreviated: if a causal route is compounded from sub-routes, and for each sub-route X–Y first there is X and then there is Y, then I will say that the causal route is *filled*.

Now consider a case in which there are various causal routes available, where more than one causal route is allowed by the laws of nature applied to the case. There will be disagreement between those of determinist and those of indeterminist sympathies as to whether any such cases actually obtain: but it is important to see what we should say about them before deciding where our sympathies lie.

Suppose the ball is released at A and ends up at H. There are different causal routes: ABDH, ABEH and ACEH. If the release of the ball at A causes its presence at H, then the ball is released at A, is present at H, there is a causal route from A to H and a causal route from A to H is filled. So the release of the ball at A causes its presence at H if, for example, the ball is at A, then at B, then at E , then at H.

If, as seems to be the case, we can pick out causal links in this set up, then that would suggest that there is no point in making it definitive of a causal link that a cause is a necessary condition of its effect, or a sufficient condition of its effect. Suppose I *do* release the ball at A and it *does* end up at H, and suppose it is agreed that releasing the ball at A *does* cause it to end up at H. Still, releasing the ball at A isn't *necessary* for its ending up at H, for had the ball not been released at A it could have been placed directly on H or on some other pin. Nor is releasing the ball at A *sufficient* for its ending up at H, since it could just as well have ended up at G or I or J. These points are, of course, hardly decisive: it might be replied that releasing the ball at A is an INUS condition of its being present at H, or that releasing the ball at A plus a number of other conditions necessitates its being present at H. But the point is just that, regardless of the merits or demerits of these replies, it is not in virtue of these notions of necessity and sufficiency, however combined, that releasing the ball at A is agreed to cause its being present at H. What establishes that causal link between being released at A and present at H is rather that the ball *is* released at A, and then *is* present at H, and there is a causal route from A to H, and a causal route is filled – for example, the ball is at A, then at B, then at E, then at H.

I hope it is agreed that it will not do to deny that releasing the ball at A *does* cause its presence at H, given that it is released at A and does end up at H. It is helpful to think here about the connection between causation and responsibility. Suppose that underneath H there is a valuable Ming vase. I release a steel ball at A, it ends up at H, and the vase is broken. Then, at least given some further conditions, I am to be blamed for breaking the vase; and that is to say that I am held responsible for breaking the vase. But if the link between my releasing the ball and the vase breaking sustains my being held responsible for the breakage, then there is a causal link too between my releasing the ball and the vase breaking. But that link includes the link between the release of the ball at A and its presence at H. If that latter link were not causal – if the release of the ball at A did not cause its presence at H – then the more inclusive link between my releasing the ball at A and the vase breaking could not be causal, and so I could not be blameable for breaking the vase. But that is unacceptable, and so the release of the ball at A *does* cause its presence at H.

Another point concerning this example. If I didn't *know* of any causal link between releasing the ball and the vase breaking, then I would be less likely to be blamed for the breakage. Suppose I had not known that there was a vase underneath H. Or suppose that the Galton Board set up with which I am familiar had been tampered with in some way, so that when I release the ball at say F, it *can* get to H – perhaps someone has wired the board magnetically so that the situation is not as normal, and what I thought was not a causal route in fact is a causal route. In that case I would be less likely to be blamed for breaking a vase underneath H by releasing a ball at F. But what knowledge is it on my part that is required for blameworthiness? Just that there is a way of getting from the release of the ball at A (or at F) to its presence at H: that is, that A (or F) and H are linked by a causal route. I do not need to know about what *must* follow, or what *will* follow, or even what will *most likely* follow from the release of the ball at A. And that dovetails with the corresponding non-epistemological point: that the release at A causing the presence at H is just a matter of the ball being released at A, being present at H, and there being a filled causal route from A to H.

Consider now another sort of example, in which there is more than one candidate cause to choose between. There is a wall in my garden. One night there is both a tornado and an earthquake. When it is all over my wall has collapsed. How would we choose whether to replace

(1) The wall fell down and the tornado blew and the earth quaked

by

(2) The wall fell down because the tornado blew and because the earth quaked

or by

(3) The wall fell down because the tornado blew; and as it happens the earth quaked too ?

Thinking about the circumstances in which we would replace (1) by (3), rather than by (2), makes clearer what is involved in a causal route's being filled, and why that is an important notion. It is plain that the causal route between high winds and the collapse of the wall is compounded of sub-routes: for example, from high winds to forces against the wall, from forces against the wall to cracked mortar, from cracked mortar to shifting bricks and so on. No doubt there will be sub-routes compounded in one causal route that are not compounded in the other. Suppose the causal route from the tornado blowing to the wall collapsing has as a stage uniform erosion at the top of the wall; suppose the causal route from the earth quaking to the wall collapsing does not have *that* as a stage, but does have (though the previous route does not have) the stage of cracks in the foundation and base of the wall. Then a situation in which we are willing, after investigation, to say that not only did the tornado blow, the earth quake and the wall collapse, but the mortar at the top of the wall was uniformly eroded while the base and foundations never cracked, would be precisely a case in which we would replace (1) by (3) rather than (2): in which we would say that the wall collapsed *because* the tornado blew, while as it happens the earth quaked too. Why is that a reasonable conclusion to draw from the information provided? Precisely because of what I have said about causes. The causal route from the tornado blowing to the collapse of the wall is filled, and the causal route from the earth quaking to the collapse of the wall is not. If the foundations and base of the wall had cracked too, then we would replace (1) by (2) rather than (3). For in that case both causal routes would be filled, and there could be no justification for replacing one *and* in (1) by *because* but not the other. So the important question here concerns causal routes, and their being filled or otherwise, which is to be decided by reference to details of the particular case: it is not necessary to consider such questions as what would have happened had the tornado blown but the earth not quaked.

Now consider another interesting type of causal situation: what one might call *kill-or-cure* causal set ups. In order to avoid some outcome I operate a cause. But the operation of the cause is risky: there is a chance that the effect which I want to avoid will be produced by the very operation of the cause by which I intend to prevent it being produced. I do not mean simply that the outcome comes about *in spite of* what I do to prevent it, but that the outcome comes about *because of* what I do to prevent it. Such kill-or-cure cases may sound unlikely without examples. Suppose a smallpox epidemic is raging in the land, so that without vaccination you have a very high chance of catching the disease and dying. I give you a small dose of smallpox as a vaccination. This greatly reduces your chance of catching smallpox and dying, it greatly increases your chance of surviving. For convenience sake I will call what I am aiming to secure (your survival) the *effect*, and what I am aiming to avoid (your death from smallpox) the *counter-effect*. Then there is some small chance that by giving you the injection I will bring about the counter-effect. Suppose this happens, and that you die *because of* the injection. How should we understand the *because* in that case? The cause (the injection) in fact makes the counter-effect *less* probable than it would have been had the cause not operated. And an appeal to counterfactuals does not seem helpful, for it is clearly not true that had I not given you the injection you would not have died of smallpox. We can in fact coherently suppose the smallpox to be so rampant that you would inevitably have died (probability = 1) had I not given you the injection. Nevertheless, it is certainly sensible to say that you died, not just *in spite of*, but *because of* the injection. There are, of course, obvious points which could be made in connection with this type of case. For example, we might distinguish among vaccinees between those who have a certain feature F and those who do not: perhaps F is some physical predisposition to be adversely affected by the vaccination. It could then be said of the F-vaccinees that the injection necessitates their developing smallpox, while administering the injection to the non-F-vaccinees has no ill effect. Once again, though, I need declare no opinion about the plausibility of such a suggestion. The differentiating factor F is just *posited*. And there is nothing objectionable in that, as such. But it *would* be objectionable if the factor were posited because it was thought to be required in order to make sense of the notion of a cause bringing about a counter-effect, while rendering that counter-effect less probable than it would have been had the cause not operated. There may be such a differentiating factor, or there may not be: but we can well understand what it is for there to be a causal link between the injection and the death we are seeking to avoid without deciding the question.

Another example is shown in Figure 2. Suppose there is international tension between ourselves and our neighbours. Our country wants peace. We reason like this. Making hostile speeches is likely to cause our neighbours to seek peace: this seems plausible – they

	Cause	Absence of cause
Effect	1	3
Counter-Effect	4	2

Figure 2.

will think that it is not worthwhile waging war against a country whose people are very ready to fight back. There is some slight chance that making hostile speeches will actually *cause* our neighbours to wage war on us: for example, their national pride might be hurt, or their leaders might think it necessary to respond strongly with action to our words, maybe with the hope that we will back down. Suppose, on the other hand, that we do not make any hostile speeches, and do nothing at all. Then there is some chance that our enemies will wage war on us, and some chance that they will seek peace. We might order the chances as in Figure 2, where *cause* is making hostile speeches, *absence of cause* is not doing so, *effect* is our enemies seeking peace and *counter-effect* is their waging war.

If we make hostile speeches it is more likely that our enemies will seek peace than that they will wage war. If we do not make hostile speeches then it is more likely that they will wage war than that they will seek peace. In this situation the rational thing to do is to make hostile speeches (or at least, we can imagine the specific values of the probabilities that give us the ordering being such as to render that the rational course to follow in order to attain what we want, namely peace).

Suppose we *do* make hostile speeches, and the unlikely outcome occurs: our enemies wage war. Then the question I am interested in is this: what would establish whether it was true that our enemies waged war *in spite of* our hostile speeches or whether it was true that our enemies waged war *because of* our hostile speeches?

If our enemies waged war, not because of, but in spite of, our hostile speeches, still it is reasonable to suppose that they waged war *because of* something – for example, because of whatever it is that is the cause of the international tension. In that case the situation is much closer to a case I have already talked about, in which there are two candidate causes for some effect (the tornado and the earthquake as candidate causes for the collapse of my wall). Suppose the cause is that they wanted our land. If we *did* make hostile speeches and they *did* want our land and they *did* wage war, and yet we want to say that they waged war *because* they wanted our land and *in spite of* our hostile speeches, then that must be on the grounds that the causal route from the making of hostile speeches to the waging of war was not filled. And that seems a highly plausible position to take, once we consider the consequences of claiming the causal route from hostile speeches to waging war and the causal route from wanting land to waging war are *both* filled, and yet that there is a causal asymmetry: that they waged war *in spite of* out hostile speeches and *because of* their desire for our land. In an example like this it is less appropriate to talk of *laws* generating or sustaining a causal route: the causal route is fixed more loosely by whatever story it is that gets us from the making of hostile speeches to the waging of war. For that causal route to be filled is for something like the following to hold: we make hostile speeches, the mass of their people come to know of them, their people are stirred to anger against us and against their own government's inaction, their government makes formal protests to us but their people continue to agitate for war, their people demand the resignation of their government and the ascent to power of a well-known hawk, their government remains in power but mobilises the army and attacks us. (If this is not plausible, then substitute any story you like as to how one gets from hostile speeches on our part to waging war on their part; and of course this is only the outline of a causal route, since each of the sub-routes I've mentioned will be compounded from other sub-routes.) Suppose we *do* make hostile speeches, the mass of their people *do* come to hear of them, they *are* stirred to anger..., and they *do* attack. If the causal route is filled in that way, then it seems incoherent to say that nevertheless they did not wage war *because* of our hostile speeches, but rather *in spite of* them. It makes no difference if there is another causal route from their desiring our land to their waging war, and that causal route is filled too. If that were so, then that would be a case in which they waged war because of our hostile speeches *and* because of their desire for our land too. On the other hand, if one of the causal routes was not filled – for example, that from our hostile speeches to their invasion, since their people never heard about our speeches, or their pride was not stung – then in *that* case we would say that they waged war *because of* their desire for our land, and *in spite of* our hostile speeches. The point, again, is that there being a causal link is just a matter of there being the cause and there being the effect, and there being a filled causal route between them.

Now this casts light on what was puzzling about kill-or-cure situations. If this is what it is for a causal link to obtain, then there is not really a puzzle about how a cause can render what it *does* produce *less* likely than it would have been had the cause not operated. The injection *is* given and death *does* occur, and the causal route from the injection to the death *is* filled: for example, the injection is given, and then there is swelling of the arm round the point of injection, and then fever develops, and then spots appear... and then the patient dies. The fact that beforehand it was highly improbable that this causal route would be filled is not relevant to the fact that the injection did cause the death; and there is certainly no reason to argue that the injection did not cause the death in that case, on the grounds that the injection did not increase the probability of death, or because death from smallpox would inevitably have occurred anyway. The injection did cause death in that, to use Elizabeth Anscombe's phrasing, death derived from, arose out of, came of, the injection. So the point of talking of causal routes and their being filled is to make clearer what the *derivedness* of effect from cause is.

It is reasonably straightforward, if these are the terms in which causality should be thought about, to say what it would be for a causal link to be a determining or a necessitating one. It cannot be right to gloss something's being a determining cause by saying that given the cause the effect had to follow, for there will always be the possibility of interfering with the cause and preventing the effect being produced.[5] It is rather to say that given that nothing interferes, then the effect has to follow from the cause. And in the terms I have been using, that would be expressed as follows: given the cause, and given that the causal route is filled, then the effect will result. How should we express the modality, that the cause *necessitates* the effect? Talk of modalities is connected with the existence of causal routes, since to say that there is a causal route from Fs to Gs is to say that Fs *can* give rise to Gs. So if the *only* causal route from Fs is to Gs, then Fs *have to* give rise to Gs if they give rise to anything. They might, of course, be interfered with and prevented from giving rise to anything at all (the causal route might not be filled), as might any determining cause be interfered with. So for a particular cause *a* to be a determining cause of its effect *b* is for it to be the case that the only causal route from *a* goes to *b*. So if you start off with *a* then if anything results it will be *b*. Suppose that the ingestion of cyanide is a determining cause of death. Then any filled causal route from the ingestion of cyanide by a man will result in the death of that man. This must be the correct thing to say about determining causes. For if there were more than one causal route, that would be to say that there would be more than one effect possible from that cause; and if that were so, then the cause could hardly be a determining cause, since given the cause it would be possible that either of the effects should result.

Finally I should say something about a problem which might strike the reader. It now seems a mystery how we are ever to establish laws of nature and causal generalisations. Usually one would answer: by experiment. I set up what I think are the right conditions, I operate the F (for example, I pour on the acid) and I see if I do indeed get the G (for example, I see if hydrogen is produced).

[5] Anscombe emphasises the importance of the notions of interference and prevention, *Collected Philosophical Papers, vol. II*, p. 147; and compare what I say with the account Anscombe gives of necessity as connected with causation, ibid., pp. 144–45.

Stephen Makin

But this might appear to be a senseless procedure, given what I have said about the connection between causal routes and causation. Suppose I operate the F in a particular set up, and the G *does* come about. Still, what grounds do I have for believing that the F *did* cause the G? For to believe that is to believe that the F operated, and then there was the G, and there is a filled causal route between them. But in this experimental case, what I am trying to find out is precisely whether there *is* any causal route between Fs and Gs.

In a concrete case I would *guess* or *assume* that the F causes the G. So, as part of that assumption, I would assume that there is a causal route between Fs and Gs, and so I would *assume* that there is some law of nature linking Fs and Gs. I can then test this law of nature to see if it coheres with what I take to be other laws of nature. For example, I might in another set-up operate an F, and see if my expectation that a G results is fulfilled. If it is not fulfilled, then I may either take it that there is no causal route between Fs and Gs, or take it that in this new set up the causal route is not filled.

The latter is the more economic assumption. So, making the assumption that in this new set up there *is* a causal route, but that it is not filled, the rational procedure is to find out in more detail what the assumed causal route is, so that I can see at what point in this set up it fails to be filled. In order to find out what the causal route is I try to find out the conditions under which it is filled. I operate an F under slightly different conditions, and see if I get a G, and I try to see what goes on as an F produces a G. This seems like a reasonable description of how one might actually go about testing putative laws; and one can see that it would be a sensible procedure given what I have said about causal links. So what I have said about causal links cannot be inconsistent with a plausible answer to the question of how we discover laws of nature.

Now it is true that in the examples I have discussed of specific causal links, I have assumed that many well-established explanatory theories are true: for it is just these theories which generate the causal routes. It is possible, of course, that some of them are not true, and so it is possible that the causal routes in the world are not as I have taken them to be. But that confirms the point I have been making about the relation between cause, effect and causal route. For if we were wrong about laws of nature, and so wrong about causal routes, then we would also hold that the *causes* in the world were not as we had taken them to be.

To sum up. We can explicate saying that there is a causal link between this F, *a*, and this G, *b*, as saying that there is *a* and there is *b*, and there is a filled causal route between them: a way of getting from *a* to *b*, with the requisite sub-stages of that route coming about. This account of a causal link does not require any decision on contentious questions about causation and modality, laws of nature, counterfactuals and so on. The neutrality of the account is not, however, purchased at the cost of its being insubstantial and vacuous. It does a good job of explaining the causal links in cases which are *prima facie* difficult for any account of causation. And the account expands on Anscombe's remark that:[6]

> causality consists in the derivativeness of an effect from its causes. This is the core, the common feature, of causality in its various kinds. Effects derive from, arise out of, come of, their causes

For the most significant point that I take from what Anscombe says is this, that the notions which will cast most light on what causality is are not those of necessity or counterfactual dependence, but something more obvious: derivativeness.

[6] Ibid., p. 136.

Intention, freedom and predictability

PETER GEACH

Elizabeth Anscombe's most important philosophical work has been on intention and action: in her book *Intention* and in many of her articles. To read *Intention* is like watching somebody hew a path with a machete through a jungle of confusion and mythology. Such work is never done, for the jungle grows apace. Here I take up some of the task.

I may take as a text for my discourse Hume's definition of will: 'the internal impression we feel and are conscious of when we knowingly give rise to any new motion of our body or new perception of our mind'. We need not dwell on the terms 'internal impression' and 'perception': we may simply gloss them by 'inner experience'. What will first concern us in Hume's definition is not what specially belongs to him, but what he here shows himself as taking for granted. Namely, that what constitutes our 'knowingly bringing about' some action of body or mind is some *other* action, an act purely of the will. In Scholastic jargon these acts purely of the will are called *actūs eliciti* of the will: other acts of body and mind such as we 'knowingly give rise to' are *actūs imperati*, acts performed at the behest of the will, and each such act derives its voluntary character from some *actus elicitus*. It does not occur to Hume, sceptical of much else, to challenge this tradition.

As to the character and content of *actūs eliciti* there have been various views. One sort of view would have the primary *actus imperatus* to be a twitch of a muscle (or perhaps, as in William James, the mental image of a twitch) and would give the name 'volition' to the *actūs eliciti* of will that evoke such twitches. I believe this survives in legal textbooks; but it has been so thoroughly exploded in recent philosophy, particularly Ryle's *Concept of Mind*, that I do not propose to discuss it.

A far more influential view has been the view that *intentions* are occurrent acts of the mind. There are immediate grounds for suspicion. It seems absurd that an intention should steal upon one unawares, like a fit of anger or fear. On the other hand, how can there be voluntary acts of intending? If an act is voluntary, one may be ordered or advised to do it; but as Wittgenstein pointed out, the verb 'to intend' has no usable imperative, one cannot use such an imperative to order or ask or advise someone to intend something.

People have sometimes identified as acts of intending what are perfectly genuine acts of the mind, namely acts of 'saying in one's heart' something like, 'What I am about (to do) is so-and-so.' But such performances will not fulfil the role of intentions. For one thing, in ever so many cases of intentional action, nothing like this is 'said in the heart' at the time. Theories of acts of intention cover up such awkward cases by such phrases as 'virtual intention' or 'habitual intention'. (There is a prayer a priest says before Mass declaring in what intention he is about to celebrate; perhaps it has been thought that the actual intention thus elicited will pass on some of its force to supplement what might be a merely virtual or habitual intention during the actual ceremony; but what if the prayer itself has become a matter of habit?) Again, as regards what I say in my heart, just as much as what I say aloud, the question may be raised whether I really meant it. This question may be terribly serious: in *Grace Abounding* Bunyan records agonies of mind as to whether he had meant the wicked words he said in his heart; probably alluding to these terrors in a time of inward peace, he records how Christian in the Valley of the Shadow took as his own inner intent what a devil was whispering to him. But something as to which we can again ask what was meant and how it was meant cannot fulfil the role of determining the way an outward act is meant.

This has had a great relevance for ethical discussions. There are two all too familiar patterns of argument, which I may give as follows

1 Intending an action in a certain way may make all the difference to the moral quality of the action.

   Intending an action in a certain way consists in saying within oneself: this is what I am about (to do).

   Ergo: Saying within oneself: what I am about (to do) is so and so may make all the difference to the moral quality of the action.

2 Saying within oneself: what I am about (to do) is so and so cannot make much difference to the moral quality of the action.

   Intending an action in a certain way consists in saying within oneself: this is what I am about (to do).

   Ergo: Intending an action in a certain way cannot make much difference to the moral quality of the action.

Logically these two arguments are on a level, related as 'P, Q, *ergo* R' and 'not R, Q, *ergo* not P'. They are valid but not sound; the premise Q is false, and so are both conclusions. The first argument is often exemplified in sophistical Catholic moralists; the second in Utilitarian moralists of various shades.

A sample sophistical argument of the first kind is used to justify killing people in war: the combatant simply 'directs his intention' away from killing to some other effect of firing his missile. 'I am firing off this bullet, property of the Republic, on a certain path within the Republic's territory.' Too bad for an invader that he is on that path! I may have every sympathy with the Republic's good soldier, but I cannot think he does his mind and soul any good by rehearsing this story to himself. Anthony Kenny gave me a versification of this:

Say I'm unlawfully aggressed:
I pull the trigger – well I'm blessed!
He hit my bullet with his chest!
I'm glad I did my morals.

As regards the second pattern of argument, the conclusion that the way you intend an action cannot make much difference to the moral quality of the action would hardly be put forward nakedly, it is too absurd; but people *are* prepared to say that the difference between intended and merely foreseen consequences cannot have much, if any, moral significance. Thus, suppose a leader of a scientific expedition has to send a subordinate on a dangerous but necessary journey: on this view it would be morally irrelevant whether the leader merely foresaw the other's death as likely or positively intended it. In particular cases like this, the importance of the distinction between intention and foresight is pretty plain; but people may get muddled by a different choice of examples and by saying that drawing the distinction only leads to Catholic sophistries about 'directing intention'.

Logically speaking, as I said, the two sorts of bad argument are on a level; both have done immense harm.

There is a genuine sort of act that is sometimes confounded with the supposed act of intention; *trying* or *setting oneself*. Let us first get this confusion out of the way. The verbs 'to try' and 'to set oneself' have usable imperatives, unlike 'to intend': cf. the 'Get set!' in athletics. 'You may not succeed, but for God's sake *try!*' makes perfect sense: 'intend' in place of 'try' would be absurd. Again, one may intend to try to do something; but hardly, try to intend to do it.

Let us see, then, whether trying, or setting oneself, can fulfil the traditional role of *actus eliciti*. Could we say that any voluntary act is preceded by an experience of *trying* to do it? Of course if the trying is both effortless and successful we wouldn't call it trying; but this may be argued to be like the way that treason which prospers may not be called treason; such linguistic proprieties ought to weigh very light in philosophy. Anyhow one could just cast around for

Peter Geach

some more acceptable expression; Prichard's 'setting oneself' might serve.

But trying or setting oneself will not fulfil the role of an *actus elicitus*. Sometimes there is no gap between the trying and the deed: 'I did it the very first time I tried.' When a man says he has tried and has failed to perform, the question must arise what his trying consisted in. Trying to do A when one does not actually do A always consists in some other voluntary act B. When with numb fingers I try to write, I may be actually holding and moving the pen; when I try to recall a forgotten name, I voluntarily call up thoughts I take to be true about that person, which I know by experience of such cases will be followed by the name's popping up in my mind.

Now if trying to do A consists in a voluntary act B, then there appears a danger of a vicious regress if B in turn has to be preceded by an act of trying. The regress in fact stops with an action which the agent simply *does*, without a distinct act of trying. Similarly, the athlete who sets himself upon the command 'Get set!' does not have to *set himself* to set himself.

Wittgenstein once remarked that philosophers who discuss the possibility of precognition never recollect that each of us knows and could say, enormously often, what he himself is just about to do. In this little realm a man is lord, *dominus*, says Aquinas: knowledge and power coincide, just as God is Lord of the world and his knowledge is cause of things.

As against this, there is the view that nobody may say 'It is up to my choice right now, whether I raise or do not raise my arm'; sudden death or palsy might always falsify the claim; anyhow, the raising of my arm depends on facts about my muscles and nervous system of which I am hugely ignorant. This, I think, is only the familiar sceptical move *from* the occurrence of error in some class of judgments *to* there being no case of knowledge in that class; no special feature of the claim to a knowing exercise of free choice is being considered.

I cannot here and now discuss and combat the general sceptical strategy. Obviously the same ploy can be used against my claim to know something because I see it is so with clear vision of what lies before me, or because I remember it; what do I know of the relevant workings of the nervous system when I see or remember something? But in fact the certainty about a particular free choice is far greater than for a claim to see or to remember something. Misrepresentations and misobservations, or again lapses and distortions of memory, are all too frequent even when one feels very certain; but it must happen only very rarely that a man's claim to be free, e.g., about moving his arm is promptly falsified by the speaker's suffering death or a stroke.

76

Intention, freedom and predictability

It is entirely futile to confine freedom of choice to freedom of decision that holds good in some inner realm even if one's body lets one down. Sceptical doubts might be raised even about this seemingly more modest claim: how can the agent know that his *mind* will not betray him by his going mad in mid-thought like Nebuchadnezzar? If free choice made a difference only to what happened in the theatre of the mind, and not in the wide world, then the will would be a chimera buzzing in a vacuum and feeding on second intentions.

Choice just is choice between alternatives, and this means there are alternative scenarios for what happens in the physical world. Poles speak of Adam's choice, of a bride that is to say; but such figures of speech are exceptions that prove the rule of what choice is. Aristotle continually refers to *ta endechomena*, to what may turn out one way or another. Unless this class has members, free choice is an illusion. The conviction that determinate futurity is alone admissible in thought has been strangely strong among philosophers. If they are Aristotelian scholars, their attempts to read this into Aristotle must be seen to be believed. (Why should he have laboured mightily to work out the logic of propositions about *ta endechomena*, if on his view all such would have to be false?) Pope wrote of God's having, while 'binding Nature fast in fate/Left free the human will': many Catholic philosophical textbooks similarly present Nature as a deterministic system *except* for interventions by Divine miracles or human free choice! Secular philosophers who think like this of course do not allow the exceptions.

That there are *ta endechomena* is of course not a sufficient condition of free choice, but it is a necessary condition. We could not act rationally without regularities in Nature we could count on; it would be like Alice trying to play croquet with live flamingoes as mallets and live hedgehogs as balls. But croquet would be equally impossible if the balls moved like stars in their courses regardless of players' choices.

The root of freedom is that a course of events envisioned in the understanding does not point to its own realisation rather than non-realisation: *idem est intellectus oppositorum*. Often it is thought that valuations tip the scale, and these are given to the agent, not chosen by him. But valuations are not like forces in dynamics. For example (here I borrow from Austin Farrer) a guest's choice of dish may be made on a scale of greater or less palatability, greater or less digestibility, or greater or less politeness: even if he took all these scales into account there could be no determinable issue.

A conspicuous example of freedom is such freedom of deliberation. Let me give an example that I believe I owe to Mabbott. Just

77

Peter Geach

as a don is about to dine in Hall, he receives an expected telephone call: he knows he can deal with it in a couple of minutes. There is no doubt that the dinner is more attractive than taking the telephone call, but he does not therefore fatally follow this stronger desire; he is able to reckon that he can take the call now and go into Hall afterwards. This is an example of freedom of deliberation, happily one that raises no misleading thoughts of a grim moral struggle. Children have much less freedom of deliberation, and therefore less responsibility for their actions.

In the very act of laying these arguments before my readers, I have been presupposing (what I hope is the case) that they enjoy some freedom of deliberation in regard to them, and that the way they regard them is not already determined by the bent of their minds. Only thus does it make sense to 'appeal to reason' – something that a denier of free will cannot consistently do. If you hold that reason is always the slave of the passions, and so-called rational considerations are only rationalisations of wishful or fearful thinking, then you cannot without self-refutation offer for rational consideration arguments designed to convince people of this. No doubt reason often is enslaved, we may often deceive ourselves that we are acting rationally when we are not; but if freedom of deliberation is a mere chimera, why do we desire such freedom - desire to appear rational in our own eyes?

To think that free choice is incompatible with our knowledge of natural regularities is a sign of various errors and confusions. The notion of 'unbroken laws' is itself highly confused; natural attributes of things issue in tendencies, not uniformly in actual kinds of event, and prevention and interference are ubiquitous, as Mill already says. Even if we waive this, unbroken laws need not exclude alternatives from the future; in Grand Master chess the laws of chess are never broken, but that does not make the course of the game predictable.

Large claims are sometimes made for the determinations of human choices by identifiable sorts of cerebral events: the claimants become cagey if asked for details. But one need not here appeal to human ignorance, even though much less is known than some spokesmen pretend. It has long been known that the neural network of ants, for example, though much simpler than ours, varies from one individual to another. There are vastly more possibilities of different neural structures between human beings. It is therefore wildly irrational to suppose that similar patterns of behaviour developed by education are determinately connected with similar patterns of neural activity in different brains: as well might one suppose that the similar external shape of two topiary peacocks corresponds to a likeness of the ramifications under the green surfaces. To pretend that deterministic neural correlates of behaviour are already established beyond serious doubt is mere bluff that ought to be called.

Appeals to physical determinism are slightly less in vogue (though by no means quite obsolete) in view of developments in subatomic physics. People who take statistical laws as the last word in physics sometimes argue that the will no more affects what statistical regularities require than what deterministic laws would require. But again the objection is confused. Any number of statistical regularities are to be observed in the speech of an Englishman or in the style of a particular English author; but one could not take seriously the idea that these regularities deny the author's freedom of self-expression: they do not dictate whether he expresses himself wisely or foolishly, writes truth or falsehood, or what truths or falsehoods he comes to utter. Free choice rides upon such regularities, and upon the statistical regularity of nature in her minute operations.

Philosophers sometimes appeal to the distinction between reasons and causes to uphold a doctrine of compatibilism; the physical causation of bodily motions does not exclude their being also describable as actions that have reasons. I see no future for this doctrine. If physical circumstances describable without reference to my intentions enabled someone to predict what sound-waves came out of my mouth, then my freedom of speech would be a mere illusion.

Freedom of choice must not be either over-dramatised or exaggerated. It is over-dramatised by those who represent each free choice as a choice between right and wrong, duty and inclination, or the like. This representation stems, I think, from the false ethical view that makes us obliged to choose the *best* alternative, rather than simply to do good and shun evil doing. To an uncaptive mind it is clear that several alternatives may each be good, with no wrong done if any one is chosen.

Freedom of choice may be exaggerated in our thought if we forget one important sort of slavery. A slave to tobacco may be free to choose whether to smoke this cigarette now, but will assuredly have smoked forty before the day is over. In this way, Aquinas says, we are slaves to sin, even, apart from grace, to mortal sin: by deliberation and forethought *each* sin could be avoided, but we cannot maintain our vigilance and avoid *all* sins.

Predicting a man's action from his settled plans in no way counts against his freedom, so long as the plans themselves were freely adopted. Of course it is an undesirable characteristic in a man to be 'unpredictable' in the sense that we cannot rely on his word and do not know what he will take into his head to do next. But from its being desirable that we can predict a man's actions given his chosen plans, it does not follow that there would be nothing objectionable about his being predictable by some 'experts' from facts outside his knowledge and control. It is one thing for John's friends to predict that he will ask Mary's hand in marriage because they divine his intentions from his actions; it is quite another thing to believe it possible to predict the marriage because of John's and Mary's horoscopes or psycho-physical types, or because John's twin brother has married a girl just like Mary. Such predictions are pseudo-science.

It really would be incompatible with freedom if there were available predictions of human actions from non-rational causes. A man's choice is only 'Adam's choice' if it is so determined. If some action on a man's part is wholly determined by, and predictable from a knowledge of, events and circumstances in the world over which the 'agent' had no control, then it is quite inappropriate to call him the agent or to count him responsible for his 'actions'. Such prediction certainly is incompatible with our account of man's freedom.

'Brainwashing' is often alleged to give evil men techniques that make such prediction possible. But 'brainwashing' does not always work in practice; and indeed it is self-contradictory to suppose that what a man says could both be reliably controlled by others and be the man's own choice. Threats, however dire, need not destroy free choice: 'Either your signature of your brains will be on this paper in five minutes' does offer an alternative to signature though a grim one. How much, if at all, we blame a man for choosing the easier alternative will depend on the circumstances, on what is at stake; but he still *has* a choice, and if his duty is to die bravely he *may* be brave. Men quite often are brave; indeed men quite often risk their lives on foolhardy feats with no call of duty.

Freedom is a great but perilous gift. Freethinkers have mocked at freedom of choice. The Victorian rationalist Sir Leslie Stephen mocked at the idea that there is a great First Cause and ever so many little first causes that can damn themselves if they so choose. But this way of speaking is not to be held wholly inept: it may be compared with what has been said sometimes by Doctors of the Church. For instance, Anselm in *De casu Diaboli* ends by saying that the only reason we can give for Lucifer's fatal misfeasance is that he willed because he willed; his willing was, so to say, its own effect and its own efficient cause. That a choice may in this way be *causa sui* is the Divine dignity given to Lucifer, as to all intellectual creatures: and God values the freedom of creatures much more than their all being happy. As Aquinas puts it, in discussing the same topic of why some of the angels fell: 'that is the way the intellectual creature was made: to act for his end was put into his free choice'. Or as Chesterton rather grimly put it: the damned wear their halos even in Hell. 'I said, you are gods; and all of you children of the Most High. But you shall come to destruction and perish like the princes.'

Intention

ROSALIND HURSTHOUSE[1]

When I first read *Intention* as a student it seemed misnamed, since, I thought, it gave an account of intentional action all right, but left me still wondering what an intention was. It was only with years of rereading that I came to see that one beauty of the account was that it eliminated the need to ask.

The full beauty of the account, I would claim, is that it is true; but its most devoted admirer could not claim that it has been generally recognised. It has been obscured by the prominence of the current causal theory according to which intentions are antecedent events which explain intentional action. Indeed I have found in discussion that some people, perhaps misled by Davidson's many acknowledgments of *Intention*'s insights, assume that all the book contains of value is some gropings towards the theory he has been developing since *Actions, Reasons and Causes*. But nothing could be further from the truth. *Intention* stands as an account of intentional action totally opposed to any causal account and not in need of radical development or improvement.

In this paper I argue that the current causal theory does not deserve its present prominence and that when we weigh up the merits of it and Anscombe's rival view it can be seen that there are powerful arguments to say that present fashion has chosen the wrong path. If Anscombe is right, the logic of statements of intention and the explanation they give is quite other than that found in the report of a cause; indeed it is, as we shall see, wrong even to ask what an intention is.

My whole attack is inspired by what I take Anscombe to say, so I refer to *Intention* constantly, thereby presupposing some familiarity with it. But I hope this paper may help some readers to understand what is, undeniably, an extraordinarily difficult book, by seeing how some of her points bear on the causal theory. Certainly, in writing it, I came to appreciate parts of *Intention* as never before.

[1] I must thank Philippa Foot, Anne Jaap Jacobson, Michael Kelar, Gavin Lawrence, John McDowell and Michael Thompson for help with earlier versions of this paper. Particular thanks are due to Michael Smith for the most patient discussions with me on the causal theory, and to Anscombe herself for much help and encouragement.

Rosalind Hursthouse

1 Some preliminary skirmishes

Of course 'the' causal theory has many versions, and the versions many exponents with their own detailed disagreements, but despite a few specific references I have tried to keep the arguments general and invite the reader to try the cap on and see if it fits.[2] I begin by giving a general version of the causalist thesis, and shall call anyone who holds it a 'causalist'.

> C: Intentional actions are actions (or movements) caused, perhaps in a certain way, by certain mental states or events, whose occurrence explains the occurrence of the action (or movement).

1 *The existence of mental causes.* It seems that Anscombe legislates against this thesis in her specification of when the question 'Why?' in its special sense is refused application. It is refused application with this sense (i.e. the answer does not give the agent's reason for acting) when the answer states a cause, including a mental cause (§16). So an answer to the question which does cite a reason, be it of the form 'I want(ed) to ...' or 'I'm trying to ...' or 'I intend(ed) to...' or whatever, cannot be citing a mental cause; hence whatever mental events or states are cited as reasons for the intentional action, they cannot be causes of it. Anscombe's ground for stipulating that when the answer to 'Why?' gives a mental cause it does not thereby give the agent's reason for acting is that if, for example, I knock a cup over because I suddenly saw a frightening face and it made me jump, I clearly did not knock the cup over intentionally and the 'because' clause does not give my reason for acting.

But this is a point which surely everyone must accept, whatever their views on reasons as causes. Anscombe's specification could be (programmatically) reformulated by a causalist as follows: the question 'Why?' is refused application when what is cited is either (i) a cause external to the agent (outside his body) or (ii) a particular sort of mental cause (viz. the sort given in the knocking over the cup example.) How one chose to fill out (ii) would of course depend on what version of C one held, and, as part and parcel of that, what one regarded as borderline or non-examples of intentional action. If you hold that intentional actions are actions caused by Xs, then your Xs may be such as to allow you to fill out (ii) as 'a particular sort of mental cause, viz. any mental cause which is not an X nor has caused an X which is the immediate cause' (e.g., trying, volitions).

[2] Some of my stalking horses: Davidson (at any rate on many people's interpretation of him) Pears, McGinn, Davis, Shaffer, O'Shaughnessy, Goldman, Audi, Danto, Honderich, Lewis, Loar, ...

Or, if not, then you might say 'viz. any mental cause which does not operate in the particular way Xs do in bringing about their effects' (e.g. beliefs + desires, intendings). Or 'viz. any mental cause whose content does not rationalise the action.'

How plausibly a particular causalist can make this move will depend on many things, not least amongst them, his account of the agent's capacity to answer the question 'Why?' and the restraints he places on the ascription of mental events and states. These are points to which I shall return later.

One reason why it is worth quoting Anscombe's views on mental causes right at the beginning is that they show that she does not deny the existence of mental events (though did anyone ever, apart from Skinner? – certainly Ryle and Wittgenstein didn't) nor even that such events may cause actions (§11).[3] What she does deny is that to cite a reason for an intentional action is necessarily to cite such an event, for, the claim is, often no such appropriate event will have occurred. In particular, 'intention' does not refer to a mental event (or state) which precedes or accompanies an intentional act and makes it intentional; there may be mental events which immediately precede intentional actions but there need not be.

2 *The logical connection argument.* Now this point about the existence of mental events which precede or accompany intentional action is, or ought to be, the fundamental disagreement between those who differ over whether reason explanations are causal. The old argument against the view that reasons are causes however was not this but the logical connection argument. Supposedly deriving its authority from Hume, the argument maintained that there could not be a (any?) logical connection between a cause and its effect, that there was such a connection between a reason and the action done because of that reason, and hence that reasons could not be causes. Another common version of the argument involved the claim that cause and effect must be 'independently identifiable'.

Despite the fact that no proponent of the argument made a point of denying that there were suitable mental events to be thus identified, the best way, I think, to understand why the old 'logical connection' argument was wielded with such extraordinary confidence despite its manifest inadequacies is to see it as embodying that conviction. No proponent of it worried about exactly why an 'independent' identification of the cause had to be available; no-one hesitated over ruling out, say, 'John's desire (volition, intention) at t' as

---

[3] Nor even that actions thus caused may be intentional. (See the discussion in §11 of my destroying a message.) Hence, I take it, causal explanations do not as such compete with reason explanations as has often been maintained.

'mere description' rather than 'identification', because everyone who deployed it was convinced in advance that frequently the putative mental items did not exist and hence could not be identified or cited as causes at all.

The untendentious claim of causal realism:

> CR: if two things are related as cause to effect there must really be two things to be thus related

involves the causalist in the claim that for every intentional action there must exist at least one antecedent (or contemporaneous) mental item to be its (at least) partial cause, and the intuitive basis for denying the causal account is the conviction that there often is no such mental item and hence that it is false to claim that there must be.

If I am right that this is the intuition that lies behind the logical connection argument then that argument *per se* was strictly irrelevant to the issue of whether reasons are causes. But, by the same token, its rebuttal plays a similarly irrelevant role in justifying causalist theories of intentional action. If what is centrally at issue is the existence of certain mental items then the claimed lack of independent description does not prove non-existence, but, equally, the availability of independent descriptions or putative identifications, such as 'the mental state with such and such causal antecedents and powers' or 'the desire to ψ' (where I can ψ by ϕ-ing), does not prove existence. It is open to anti-causalists to claim that these frequently fail to refer to or identify anything.

3 *The argument from strict introspectability.* The old argument against the existence of the mental items hypostatised by causalists was that they did not show up in consciousness. In line with this move Anscombe in *Intention* contrasts cases in which the two sentences 'I ϕ-ed intentionally' and 'I *felt* a desire to ...' are both true, with cases in which only the first is true, (§11) taking this to show that in the latter cases there cannot have been a desire to... which was the (mental) cause of the intentional ϕ-ing. She is still employing this strategy in the more recent *The Causation of Action*. Here she describes a case in which introspection fails to reveal any mental item, and the point of this is to show that in this case there is no distinct psychological state (or event) existing prior to or contemporaneously with the action to be the intention which caused it.[4]

But, for many people, this argument, call it the argument from

---

[4] *The Causation of Action* in *Knowledge and Mind*, ed. Ginet and Shoemaker, pp. 179–80.

strict introspectability, has ceased to have bite. The failure to be moved by it comes about in at least two different ways.

On the one hand there are those, like Fodor, who think that only old Cartesians need to maintain that mental items are items of which the owner is necessarily aware (or potentially aware). The science of the mind may properly quantify over items of which no consciousness has, perhaps even could, ever be aware, or over items of which, as it happens, we are sometimes aware, but animals, who have them too, never are. These 'mental scientists' have, I take it, no particular interest in people's sincere first person remarks about themselves, nor more generally in constraining the ascription of mental items in line with the dictates of commonsense psychology. One might, I suppose, think it possible that everything we say about ourselves is false and that genuine explanations will elude us until science is more advanced, but until science starts to come up with some appropriate goods I think we can put this view on one side as requiring too much investment in optimism about what future generations are going to achieve.

On the other hand there are many more moderate causalists who maintain that (at least some sorts of) mental items are always conscious or potentially conscious, *but* who accept slightly less direct proof of consciousness than strict introspectability. So, for instance, it might be said against Anscombe's above move, that I *was* conscious of a desire to φ at the time I φ-ed, not in the sense that I felt it, but in the sense that I knew or believed that I wanted to φ, or that I had a pro-attitude towards φ-ing at the time. This kind of mental state, unlike, it is said, the mental state of felt desire, is not an experience on the *basis* of which we say that we desire, but one of which we are conscious all the same. (Our frequent consciousness of such states contrasts with our occasional unconsciousness of them, as when we sincerely disavow desires which perhaps psychoanalysis would make us aware of.) Similarly, it might be said that my knowledge of the fact that I am, say, raising my arm intentionally (rather than feeling it go up willy nilly) is, or manifests, my consciousness of the mental event of my intending or willing or trying to raise my arm. Or, considering expressions of intention for the future; my ability to say what I intend to do or will do tomorrow may be said to manifest my consciousness of my present desire, or intending, to do whatever it is.

That there can be such a range of differing views about what I am, in this sense, conscious of, might be regarded as an objection to this position. But how can it be made out as an objection? If I am already convinced that very few of the causalists' hypostatised mental items exist of course I shall regard the various disagreements as

Rosalind Hursthouse

symptomatic of the fact that there is no truth of the matter here, on which agreement might converge. But if I am not already convinced, the range of differing views indicates to me only that we haven't got at the truth yet.

So, pending further argument, points about consciousness do not carry the field. However, I note here that I expect more moderate causalists to be open to what I'll call the argument from soft introspectability, meaning by that that unlike the 'mental scientists' they can be moved by considerations drawn from commonsense psychology and people's sincere first person remarks. I hope to move them in sections 2 and 3 below.

4 *The argument from Intention* §19. This section is summarised in the Contents of *Intention* as, 'We do not mention any extra feature attaching to an action at the time it is done by calling it intentional. Proof of this by supposing there is such a feature.' If this is what §19 achieves then it should, surely, provide an entirely general argument against any version of the causalist thesis, an argument, moreover, that does not depend on either strict or soft introspectability. For according to C, we do mention such a feature, namely the cause of the action, whatever, given the particular version of C involved, this happens to be (a willing or volition, an intention, a particular belief+desire pair, an all out judgment...). But no causalist, as far as I know, has ever attempted to block the argument in §19. This may be because it is so difficult to understand. There are still details of it that I do not understand myself, but it has a general drift which is readily comprehensible and which ought to give any causalist qualms.

Roughly, the argument from §19 runs as follows: Any feature, let us call it I, which is supposed to be the feature in virtue of which what someone does is an intentional action must have a particular content which relates suitably to the action, determining which intentional action is performed (first premise; agreed ground). But (second premise) nothing about the agent considered by himself at the moment of acting could possibly determine that content, which therefore might be anything, which is absurd.

Arguments for the second premise that 'nothing about the agent considered by himself at the moment of acting could possibly determine the content' of the I take us into deep issues in the philosophy of language. Anscombe gives one in *The Causation of Action*. Suppose that something about the man – say his brain states or his mental state(s) – does determine that his I has a particular content, say about a bank's opening hours. Then it must be possible for the man's I, determined in that way, to have that same content even if he has never heard of banks or clocks.[5] Which is absurd. Briefly, in terms of a post-*Intention* slogan, if meanings aren't in the head then *I*s aren't either; hence no *I* can be a state of (or event in) an agent such that solely in virtue of it and his movements he performs a certain intentional action. People unmoved by this implicitly general argument may still be bothered at least by *de re I*s. Suppose my *I* is about *that* spot, the one I have my eye on; if its having that content is determined solely by how things are with me, it must be possible for it to have the same content even if I am looking at a different, albeit qualitatively identical spot.[6]

Versions of this argument are, I think, just beginning to stir up a little mud in the causalists' pond, but since it is so involved with the philosophy of language it would be unreasonable to expect it to strike people as devastating immediately. So, *pro tem*, I commend it to causalists' attention in the expectation that it will give rise (merely) to extensive interior redecorating, but in the hope that it may eventually bring about demolition. In the meantime I shall try for a less global anti-causalist argument.

2 A new argument against the causalist thesis

Let us grant, for the moment, (a) that reason explanations are causal, (b) that a reason for an action consists of a belief and a desire, and hence (c) that there are such mental states as beliefs and desires. This, it is agreed, cannot be the whole story for it leaves unexplained why, on a particular occasion, one particular belief+desire set was causally operative while all the others were not. Or, in simple terms, I have reasons for doing many more things than whichever one, at the time, I do. So, on the causalist thesis, some further mental antecedent is needed. This apparently simple problem conceals two extremely difficult ones – well, perhaps they are just two very difficult aspects of the same problem.

Viewed one way, the problem is this: my reasons, that is my beliefs and desires, are states or dispositions that are not in themselves causally active. So the causal explanation of an action, a particular event, which cites them, must be appealing implicitly to some triggering event which brought them into play; so there must always be an explanation of why I φ-ed just then, when I did.

Viewed another way, the problem is this: my reasons form an enormously rich causal potential. Given its causal states and dispositions, a bridge, or an engine, is causally primed to do a fair

[5] *The Causation of Action*, pp. 182–3.
[6] Cf. Gareth Evans, *The Varieties of Reference*, Chapter 6.

number of things, but I, with all my beliefs and desires, am ripe to do an incalculable number. And so there must always be an explanation of why I do just *this* thing I do do, rather than just *that*.

Before considering possible causalist responses to this problem, let us see what an Anscombian would say about it. Simply, for an Anscombian, there is no problem here. I put on the kettle. Why? To make tea. Why did I put the kettle on just then, when I did? There are at least two ways in which there might be *and fail to be* answers. (i) 'A mental cause is what someone would describe if he were asked the specific question: what produced this action, what did you see or hear or feel, or what ideas or images cropped up in your mind and led up to it?' (§11). This specific question might have an answer – 'I felt a sudden desire for tea', 'You asked for some', – but it does not have to have one. 'One might shrug or say "I don't know that there was any definite history of the kind you mean"' (§11). (ii) There might be an answer which gave a reason, e.g. 'It was nearly 4p.m. and one should always have tea at 4' or 'You asked for some and you would have thought it rude of me not to respond, wouldn't you?' And this would show that I intentionally put on the kettle at five to four, or just then, when I did. But there are often no such answers. When I am doing things to a timetable – preparing meals, catching trains – I will often do them at a particular time intentionally. When I do things in response to other events – answer questions, fulfil requests – I will often do them right then intentionally. When I am engaged in an activity, such as driving or playing tennis, a lot of what I do, such as signalling or changing gear, will be done in response to other events and done when they are done intentionally. But often things are not like this, and I may have no answer to 'Why did you do that exactly then, when you did?'

What about my doing just *this* thing I do do, rather than that? For example, what about my putting on the kettle rather than making a telephone call, supposing that I have reason to do both? Well, 'φ-ing rather than ψ-ing' is just another action description and as such, an action can be intentional under that description or not. Anscombe nowhere considers this particular form of the 'Why?' question ('Why φ rather than ψ?'), but clearly answers such as 'φ-ing is better' or 'ψ-ing is ruled out' would show the action to be intentional under that description, whereas, e.g., 'It never occurred to me to ψ' or an expression of surprise at the suggestion that one might ψ (at this moment or indeed at all) would count as on a par with the answer, 'For no particular reason'. (The constraints on the truthfulness or sincerity of such rejections would be very similar to those on the man who, pumping the poisoned water, says he is only earning his pay. Why earn it that way rather than some less irresponsible way, is of course what one wants to ask.) So sometimes there will be an explanation of why I did one thing rather than another, and sometimes not, and in the latter cases, no reason why there should be (pending the constraints on sincerity of course).

So, for Anscombe, 'the problem' that I have reasons for doing far more things than, at any particular time, I do, is not a problem at all. The explanations of the actions are not made out to be causal, so there is no worry about a triggering event which explains why the action was done just then; the beliefs, desires or whatever are not made out to be ubiquitous antecedents of the actions whose sudden causal supremacy calls for further explanation. Now let us see what a causalist has to say.

Consider me at a particular moment in time; I am intentionally writing the word 'action'[7]... or rather, to be more specific about the moment, I am writing the letter 'a'. Speaking broadly and crudely, we can say that this action, my writing the letter 'a', is caused by my desire to write 'action' and my belief that to do so I must write 'a', 'c', 't', etc. Since I have many other beliefs and desires which would explain my doing all sorts of other things but which are not issuing in my writing 'a', this is far too crude, so we must narrow it down a bit; let us say that that belief and desire have somehow caused the intention to write 'action' and *this* causes me to write 'a'. But then things change; having written 'a', I then write 'c'. What can have caused that? It cannot be the same mental set, for now a different action has been caused. But a difference in the mental states seems easy to find. Before I wrote 'a' I did not, given that I know how to spell, believe that now was the moment to write 'c', given that I want to write 'action'. But when I have written 'a', I then acquire the belief that now is the moment to write 'c' and hence, or thereby, the intention to write 'c', and so on for the rest of the word.

Having taken my writing of 'a' for granted, and considered in a little depth what must be the causal antecedents of my writing 'c', let us go back to my writing of 'a'. This, we said, was caused by my intending to write 'action'. But what was I doing the moment before I wrote 'a'? Well, perhaps I was writing the 'e' of 'the', and an as yet unmentioned cause of my actions is my intention to write the sentence 'Consider the action of writing the letter "a"'.

More broadly, let us go back further in time and consider the sequence of events involving my bodily movements that preceded my writing 'a'. I make tea, I put it by the desk, I collect books and papers from around the house, I sit down at my desk; I pick up my pen, make a scribble with it, and then write 'Action' at the top of the page. All of

[7] Readers familiar with Davidson's paper on *Intending* may wish to compare his description of this example on pp. 88 and 96 of *Actions and Events*.

this could be described rather generally as 'getting ready to write a paper on action' or even, given a suitable context, as 'writing a paper on action' ('What are you doing this morning?' – 'Writing a paper'), and thereby it can be said to be caused by my intention to write a paper on action. But, as before, we must suppose that this intention remains constant throughout all the many changes in my actions, and so other things are needed to account causally for the changes.

Suppose, as above, that each temporal segment of the big action which is itself an action is caused by my belief that now is the moment to do whatever it is. But how, if I am rational, could I possibly have come by such a belief? Of course it is true that if I am to write 'action', I must write the 'c' of 'action' after I have written its 'a', not before, and, moreover, immediately, before I write its 't'. But it is not at all true that if I am to have my books about me I must collect *Intention* before I look for *Essays on Actions and Events*, nor that I must do either of these before I do all, or some, of the things I do in order to make tea. And given that I must know this is not true, how could I, aware of the fact that I have picked up *Intention*, come to believe thereby that now is the moment to hunt for a different book, or put a cup on the teatray, or whatever it is I do do next?

The trouble with any causal account which tries to make the determining event propositional in some such way (e.g. the acquisition of a belief that now is the right moment, or of an attitude about what is best all things considered, etc.) is two-fold. (a) Such a judgment would usually be false, and (b) we would ascribe to the agent reasons for ϕ-ing exactly when he did, and for ϕ-ing rather than ψ-ing, which he usually would not have. (At the time that I put the cup out I don't usually have a reason for doing that *just* then, nor for doing that rather than picking up a book.) Suppose that this 'judgmentalist' account required only that I come to believe or have an attitude about what is good (not best)? Then these two problems are avoided, but at the cost of putting us back where we started. Intending to assemble tea, books and papers, I presumably have the appropriate pro-attitudes to doing each thing necessary towards this end; that the attitudes change as I act might be appealed to to explain why I don't do anything twice, but they cannot, being all on a par, explain why I do one thing just then, and instead of another.

Is there some non-propositional sort of event which could do the same job while avoiding these pitfalls? Well, suppose it were said that the determining event was more like an imperative; say a volition, or an intention to do it *now*. Against this, I think, something very like the old Rylean objection holds. *If* this event or suddenly formed state is to do the job it is supposed to do – i.e. explain why from the great sea of causal potential, just *this* action emerged – its emergence must not be as mysterious as that of the action. But surely it is. Volitions or intentions about *now* come from the same sea; just as it is mysterious why my mental set suddenly produces, e.g., my putting the cup on the tray instead of, say, my going to look for *Intention*, it is mysterious why it suddenly produces the will to make those movements requisite for putting the cup on the tray rather than the will to make some other lot of movements. Of course, a volitionist might borrow from the judgmentalist the idea of practical reasoning as a set of mental events which determine a suitably particular volition – but then his account becomes a mere variant of the judgmental one and acquires the faults that the non-judgmental nature of volitions or whatever had supposedly avoided.

Could someone go for a mixed strategy? Suppose, that is, that the causalist bids up some mental subset as far as seemed plausible, in terms of say, formed intentions to do certain things within the next day or hour, and some conscious or unconscious mental events, such as twinges of conscience, surges of desire, noticings (of cups, books, unpaid bills), and then maintained that the rest of the channelling is done by random, or not so random, firing of neurons (or some such). 'Not so random' because in such an account one might need to say that I did the actions that made up making the tea in that order from force of habit, and think of this in terms of a sort of ingrained neural process which, once triggered by my, say, intending to make tea now, proceeds in a certain way unless interrupted by some other suitable event.

This perhaps is too much of a mere sketch for it to be clear what could be said against it, but I think the fatal question is: are these neural events identical to/correlated with mental events or not? If so, then how does this count as a *mixed* strategy? Surely no more than lip-service has been paid to the initial premise that it is downright implausible to ascribe certain mental states or events; for in appealing to neural ones which are identical to/correlated with mental ones the latter *have* been ascribed. This shows, I think, that sensitivity to the argument from soft introspectability is an untenable halfway house; we must accept strict introspectability or nothing. For without the constraint of strict introspectability, what is to block the ascription of the downright implausible mental states? Suppose one hypothesises a sort of neural firing which tends to go on in right-handed people which helps to explain (combined with subliminal noticings and lots of standing intentions) such events as my reaching for the cup (near my right hand) before I turn to pick up the jug (far left). Then what, bar strict introspectability, blocks hypothesising the belief 'it is better to reach for things near one's right hand than one's left'? Or suppose one hypothesises some sort of well-worn causal track to explain what is done as part of a familiar task, like tying one's shoelaces. What blocks ascribing a complex set of intentions and beliefs that now is the moment to move this finger that way? Of course there are *some* suggested constraints, but they are nothing like strong enough to do the job that many causalists clearly want. (i) Beliefs must have certain causal histories; well, I acquired the relevant set when I learnt to tie my shoelaces. (ii) Beliefs must be expressible in language; well, the belief that I must move this finger that way now is expressible in language if I am allowed demonstratives (and I shall be in a poor way in respect of my beliefs about people's faces and voices if I am not). (iii) The ascription of beliefs is constrained in some general way by the requirements of rationality. But unclarity about what these are is what has landed us in the present problem. If we think of the belief that the way I am tying my laces is the one and only way I can tie them to achieve my end as related to my other beliefs, such as the belief that I could equally well do it differently, the rationality requirement blocks the ascription, just as it blocks the ascription of many beliefs that it is better to φ now than to do something else (including not-φ). But *if* we think of such beliefs as necessary to rationalise actions, to make them rational in the way they clearly are, and *if* we think the beliefs are the actions' causally explanatory antecedents, rationality requires that we do ascribe them.

Suppose the causalist sticks with a genuine mixed strategy, denying that the channelling neural events are identical to or correlated with mental ones. This surely commits him to saying that the real immediate causes of many intentional actions are not mental events after all. But if he says that, can he still count as a causalist? How is his view to be distinguished now from a quite common one that any non-Cartesian might share, viz. that perhaps one day neurophysiologists will be able to trace detailed causal chains that terminate in intentional actions, chains that contain no gaps? The causalist addition to this claim is that any such chain must contain events or states identical to or correlated with mental events or states; and isn't this just what has been given up? Well, the claim might still be made: the mental neural events could be made out to lie a bit further back down the chain than was originally supposed. But now the claim, as a causalist one, has lost its point, which was to distinguish intentional from non-intentional actions, for clearly the latter too could be supposed to have mental neural events or states somewhere on their causal chain. I am thinking not only of the standard examples of deviant causal chains but also of certain unintentional reactions (guilty starts, involuntary smiles, recoils of disgust) whose explanations would mention beliefs and/or desires.

It would be, I think, quite impossible to patch this up into a causalist strategy, i.e., a position which purports to draw a distinction between intentional and non-intentional actions in terms of their causal antecedents, for once it is allowed that non-mental neural events can cause intentional actions, we lose the guarantee that mentalist considerations can dictate to the neurophysiologist which causal chains are non-deviant, and which neural events are the 'right sort' to cause intentional actions.

Finally, it might be noted that both the genuine and lip-service mixed strategies leave me oddly helpless with respect to my own actions. I am asked what I am going to do tomorrow and, to be generous, let us suppose that I don't merely have lots of beliefs and desires and intentions to do things *some* time in the future, but have actually managed to form a number of specific intentions about what to do tomorrow; pay the milk bill, write home, ring John, etc. Now (*ex hypothesi*) having formed these intentions I am able to report on them and say 'I intend to...'. But surely I can't say 'I'm going to...' without adding a very odd 'if' clause. It's not only that I'm going to if I remember and if I'm (ordinarily) able (don't die, or get flu, etc.) and if I don't change my mind but, as it were, I'm going to if my mind or brain will come up with the goods. Having formed the intentions to do all these things, many of which do not involve my having done one before the other, I can only hope that the next day some series of non-conscious onsets of belief and desire, or some collection of neural events, will occur and carry me safely through. Moreover, given the way in which descriptions of intentional actions swallow one another up, this is not a problem peculiar to what I'm going to do, but affects what I'm doing now. How can I be sure that what I'm doing now is making tea when all I have done so far is put the kettle on? The rest is not only up to nature, but on whether some suitable mental and/or neural event will prompt me to put the tea in the pot *now*.

To sum up, it is fatal to view the mind as a vast sea of causal potential from which intentional actions spring. On such a view, given the commonsense premise that I have reasons for doing many more things than whichever one, at the time, I do, there are just far too many causal antecedents to action around.

The existence of mental items. Now I maintain that the really fundamental fault here is the existence claim – the thought of all these beliefs, desires, intentions or whatever as already there, existing in the mind – which, given causal realism, is required by the causalist claim.

What is the argument for their existence?

It might be thought to be no more than causal realism plus the argument for the causalist thesis. But actually there isn't, in the literature, an argument for the causalist thesis. The only one that is standardly given, i.e. that the 'because' in 'He ɸ-ed because he wanted x/believed that ɸ-ing was a means to x' is not equivalent to 'and', shows only that a reason for action explains the action. This leaves open whether the sort of explanation is event-causality or whether the 'because' is one of Aristotle's other three 'becauses', for instance, the teleological one.[8]

If anything, the dependency of people's confidence in the existence and causalist claims is the other way around; it just seems obvious that these mental items exist and their existence argues the correctness, whatever its apparent difficulties, of the causal thesis. (That is, if there really are all these things around as antecedents to action, it is hard to see how explanation in terms of them could be anything but causal (at least in part).) So I do not think that I can carry the above argument against the causalists any further at the moment. Though I hope to have worried them, they may still plausibly think that the theory can be modified in such a way as to meet the objections. So I shall now turn to another anti-causalist argument.

3 Practical Knowledge

I now turn to consider what sort of account causalists on the one hand, and Anscombe on the other, can give of 'practical knowledge', where we take this phrase to mean my knowledge of my intentional actions – of what I'm doing or going to do. There is not much discussion of my knowledge of my intentional actions in causalist literature. No doubt this is in part because of the emphasis there on action explanation, and third person explanation to boot. Given this emphasis, it is perhaps worth pointing out that when an agent answers a 'Why?' he could alternatively just give a

[8] Nor need we take it as settled that Aristotle's four exhaust the field. McDowell has argued that the post-Wittgensteinian task for philosophy of mind is to describe how the mind (or the mental) fits into the world by giving a genuinely post-Cartesian account of the mental *and* of the world. The latter would involve, for a start, rejecting the 'imperialism of the natural sciences' – the idea that the only genuinely objective facts are those which the sciences can describe. Part of this programme could involve rejecting the dominance of the physical notion of causality. Why should an action 'because' have to be validated in *any* way by a scientific 'because' connecting neural events with the macroscopic movements of our matter?

further description of what he is doing. Moreover, the constraints of commonsense psychology dictate that the agent, though not immune to errors arising from, say, self-deception and misperformance, knows what he is doing in a way that his observers do not. (He doesn't need the clues of plans to know whether he is building a boat or a chair; though of course he may have misidentified the plans and be in error over what he is doing; nor does he need the clues of addressed envelopes to know whether he is writing to John Smith or John Jones when he writes 'Dear John'; though of course he may be deceiving himself about that.)

I shall assume that the above is agreed ground and hence that there are two points of Anscombe's which are generally accepted, viz. (i) that there is such a thing as practical knowledge, i.e., the agent's knowledge of his intentional action, of what he is doing, which is (ii) special in virtue of being non-observational.[9] But the agent's intentional action is something that happens in the observable world and hence can also be known by observation by the agent (or indeed by anyone else (cf. §4)). Anscombe claims that this creates a difficulty (§29) namely 'if there are two ways of knowing here, one of which I call knowledge of one's intentional action and the other of which I call knowledge by observation of what takes place, then must there not be two objects of knowledge? How can one speak of two different knowledges of exactly the same thing?' I am not sure that the difficulty has been correctly identified, for we are not tempted to find a similar difficulty in the two different knowledges I may have of the position of my limbs or of what startled me. Rather, *the* difficulty that strikes people is, how *can* I have non-observational knowledge of what is happening in the world beyond my body? How can I know without observation that I am painting

---

[9] 'Special in virtue of being non-observational' is my phrase, not Anscombe's, but I think uncorrupting. Her use of the phrase 'known without observation' has generated some puzzlement (Vesey *et al.* in *Analysis*), but (a) much of this has centred on her applying it to my knowledge of the position of my own limbs rather than my knowledge of my intentional actions (and she has responded – *Collected Papers,* Vol. II no. 7) and (b) at least some of it I think is spurious. Let us agree indeed that when you see me standing at the bus stop you do not observe me going to the opera though you may know that that is what I am doing. And let us agree indeed that I observe the bus-stop sign and have observed my watch and will observe the bus and could hardly be intentionally catching a bus to the opera if this were not so. So perhaps the difference between first person and third person knowledge of intentional actions is not perfectly captured by a contract between observational and non-observational knowledge. But I do not know of a better expression and this one at least now has a familiar use in this context.

a wall yellow (§28) or cutting cheese (rather than, say, butter) 'and similarly for all sorts of actions: any actions, that is, that are described under any aspect beyond that of bodily movements' (§28). For, thinking of knowledge as 'speculative', i.e., derived from the objects known, it seems obvious that unlike my knowledge of the position of my own limbs which derives directly from their position, my knowledge of the colour of the paint, or the presence of cheese must be derived from those objects *via* my observation of them.

So what are we to say? A number of positions are available. (i) We could simply give up the idea that the agent has any special knowledge of his own intentional actions (a position that might be held by Fodor-type mental scientists). I shan't discuss that position. (ii) We could give up the claim that the agent's special knowledge is special in virtue of being non-observational. I don't know of anyone who has tried that, so I won't discuss it either. (iii) The favoured way is to modify the original premise that the agent has non-observational knowledge of what takes place in the observable world. That is, the premise is modified to the claim that what the agent really has non-observational knowledge of is his intention or volition or trying.

But isn't that simply position (i)? Clearly not according to a drastic version of (iii), namely that in which 'actions' are inner and not happenings in the observable world at all. But less drastic versions of (iii) also seem consistent with holding that the agent has special knowledge of his intentional actions in some sense. We can extend the agent's non-observational knowledge to encompass his knowledge of his making such movements as he believes will result in (or constitute or contribute towards ...) his painting the wall yellow or whatever. This has the advantage of getting the object of knowledge out into the observable world, but it has another obvious weakness, namely that, if this is to be a *general* account of agent's practical knowledge, it must assume that every intentional action involves movements about which the agent has appropriate beliefs. I would add to the standard counterexamples (speaking sentences, tying shoelaces, piano trills, riding a bike, etc.) such actions as require concentration on movements some distance from one's body. Anscombe gives an instructive example in §30, where what I have to concentrate on is not the movement of my arm, but the movement of a mechanism I am trying to keep level; others would be trying to pick up a small object with two six foot sticks and various slot machine games in which I have to operate levers. Even if a believer in basic actions were unimpressed by the counterexamples there is still an oddity about this version (as a way of avoiding (i)), namely that the agent's special knowledge doesn't extend very far. It's not only that I lack non-observational knowledge that I am painting a wall yellow, but further I lack non-observational knowledge that I am painting and that I am wielding a brush. An obvious response to this suggests another version of (iii) which does not rely on the existence of 'basic actions'. This would be to maintain that the agent's knowledge of his intentional actions has two components, one observational, of what is happening, the other of his intention.

We should note that this position still resembles position (i) in that it denies that the agent has *special* knowledge of his intentional *action*, with its aspects that go beyond bodily movements. I myself count this as a strong objection to the position since I take it as a premise that the agent does have special knowledge (when he *does* know) of what he is *doing* which will be (when he does know) what is *happening*. But obviously some people don't mind giving up that idea, and I suppose they might even try explaining why we have it by appeal to the fact that when I say straight out that I am painting the wall yellow I am not in any way conscious of having put together two different bits of knowledge; *ex hypothesi* they are not the sorts of 'bits' that one can usually separate out. So I'll allow *pro tem* that the agent's special knowledge is restricted to his mental states (and perhaps the bodily movement).

However the agent's special knowledge of his intention can't be all that is needed, for, once again, there are frequently too many available candidates. I write 'Dear John'; I know I am writing to John Smith, not John Jones. But this is not captured by saying I know I intended or am intending to write to Smith not Jones, for I have decided to spend the morning on correspondence and am intending to write to each of them. But any causalist will say that what is missing here is the causal efficacy of the items I have special knowledge of. Intending to write to Smith and to Jones (and aware of this fact) I am, further, sensitive in some way to which of these intentions is causally operative as I write 'Dear John'.

Varying accounts might be given of this sensitivity and I don't want to quibble about it. Rather, I want to raise the question of when, according to causalists, it can fail me. Causalists often claim as a virtue of their account that it can attach a sense to the agent's being mistaken about his intentional action in a way other than through misperformance (e.g. my painting the wall blue when I think I'm painting it yellow) and that this is required by common-sense psychology.

For instance, I can make mistakes in, let us say vaguely, 'the areas with which psychotherapy deals'. I sincerely believe that in moving this object (taking away this pen, putting your pen on the shelf, tidying your things away...) I am trying to be helpful. I'm right about the causal efficacy of the intentions to move this object, take away this pen, etc. but wrong about the final one. I'm not intending to be helpful (? – well, if I am, that intention did not causally contribute towards this action); I'm intending to punish you for leaving your things around, and that is the intention which was causally efficacious. Whatever the details of disagreement about how far-reaching self-deception and rationalisation can be, they count, I assume, as the exception rather than the norm. That is, normally I am sensitive to the causal efficacy of my intentions (to move this object, take this pen, etc.), though in certain roughly predictable areas (for instance those involving strong emotions), I am liable to go wrong. As long as it is agreed that the possibility of this sort of error is limited in this unspecifiable but readily recognisable way anyone, causalist or not, might agree. It is no part of Anscombe's view that error through self-deception is impossible.

Another example often given is that of post-hypnotic suggestion. Roughly, I am told under hypnosis that, after I have woken up and at a certain cue, I will do something, say go to the front door, or touch a certain spot on the wall, and on cue I do so. Here, it is said there is the possibility that I believe I am collecting the post or finding out if I could reach the spot, but be mistaken. I did not move because of those intentions but because of the hypnotic suggestion. What matters here is not what actually happens in these cases (what sorts of things one is told to do and does, or how one reacts), but what causalists imagine happens. If we are imagining cases of possible error it presumably must be the case that the agent is not surprised by finding himself doing whatever it is but comes out with sincere straightforward explanations of what he is up to. If that's the way things are, then clearly I don't have to be mistaken for (on the causalist story) the post hypnotic suggestion might have induced the relevant causes whose presence and efficacy I report on in the normal way. But, it might be said, pre-theoretically we do think there is a difference between a case in which the hypnotic suggestion does that, and the cases in which they occur in the ordinary way. Well, everyone can agree to differences between cases where I do things at a particular time because of hypnotic suggestion and cases where I do things at a particular time with no such explanation, but what mistake about my intentional action do we imagine me making in the hypnosis case? That I think (wrongly) that I did it just then because it happened to occur to me to (whereas *ex hyp* it didn't 'just happen' to occur to me)? But that is a mistake about the aetiology of the occurrence of a thought, not about my action. More strongly, it might be said that we think there is a difference between the case in which the hypnotic suggestion induces the usual causes and a case in which it actually does cause the movement and the relevant mental items are quickly manufactured *post hoc*.

This, however, does not seem to be a pre-theoretically held belief from commonsense psychology. Indeed I doubt that it is coherent even in causalist terms. What is it for 'the suggestion to cause the action' but not via the medium of some relevant mental items? Well, I suppose one theoretical answer is that the hearing and understanding of the words causes some neural event which is not identical to or correlated with any mental event and it causes the movement. But this supposition takes us to the next sort of example.

This is a sort standardly used to discredit the 'contextual' theory. It can be the case, it is claimed, that the agent has reasons for φ-ing, perhaps even intends or has decided to φ (i.e. certain mental events have occurred) and φs but does not φ because of those mental items but because of something else (a muscular spasm, a neural paroxysm) which somehow makes the φ-ing not intentional. Now I hold no particular brief for the contextual theory but surely such examples do not begin to discredit it unless we assume that the agent doesn't notice anything odd. If, as his arm goes up or his finger moves, he is surprised to find that, as it were, his body has done what he was just about to do, no contextualist would claim that nevertheless he did signal, or check the king or whatever, and that our thus describing his behaviour *in the context which includes his surprise* fits it into some familiar pattern. Quite the contrary. So to make the examples work we must assume that the agent doesn't notice anything odd.

But if we suppose there are such examples, what is to be said about them in relation to the agent's knowledge? It appears that they are examples of quite 'normal' occasions (no hypnosis, not the sort of area in which self-deception flourishes) in which everyone, the agent included, thinks he is intentionally signalling or checking the king or fetching the post and is quite wrong. Now this supposition that we can be wrong in *normal* cases introduces an entirely new move.

The postulation of deviant causal chains has the same upshot. Offered examples of these do not figure in criticisms of the contextual theory (though presumably they could) and tend to be described as though the agent did or would notice the 'real' cause of his movement. But nothing in the specification of a deviant causal chain as such limits the ultimately efficacious event to being the sort that one notices, such as being shocked or unnerved. It might well be something that passed unnoticed, so, once again, it can be the case that we all thought I was intentionally bidding for Lot 29 or killing my father and were all wrong, myself included.

Rosalind Hursthouse

Now the startling point here is that there is, moreover, nothing to block the supposition that this is going on most or perhaps all of the time, nor even, I think, anything that makes this supposition one whit less likely than its alternative.

With hindsight, one might see this outcome as inevitable. For the causalist specification of an intentional action is of something with certain (non-deviant) causes which, ex hypothesi, are not accessible to strict introspection (see Section 1 above). So the possibility of error was built in at the beginning. But the possibility here is of a particularly undermining sort. The putative causes themselves (beliefs, desires, intentions...) are specified, albeit roughly, as things which play this causal role. So if the (causalist version of the) concept of intentional action can fail to have application in the real world so too the concepts of belief desire, intention. We think we frequently know that we intend or desire or believe and we're wrong.

Anscombe's position raises no such difficulties.

The account of practical knowledge which is given in *Intention* has, I think, been almost universally misunderstood, for its essential feature has been overlooked. This is that practical knowledge is not 'speculative', i.e. not 'derived from the objects known' but rather is 'the cause of what it understands'. (§48). This latter cryptic phrase and the claimed contrast it marks with speculative knowledge have been ignored, concentration having centred on Anscombe's other claim that practical knowledge is non-observational, like the knowledge I have of the position of my limbs. We shall see that its resemblance to the latter is actually incidental.[10]

Any causalist account of practical knowledge, as I noted at the outset, works initially from the assumption that my knowledge of my intentional actions, in so far as I have it, is 'derived from the objects known'. The object of knowledge is then respecified in such a way as to (try to) meet the requirements that (a) 'the' knowledge is at least in part non-observational and (b) that it can still plausibly be called 'knowledge of one's intentional action'.

Anscombe's strategy is entirely different. The 'object' remains straightforwardly the agent's intentional *action* – a happening that takes place in the observable world; and the knowledge remains all of a piece, non-observational. What she gives up is the idea that any piece of knowledge has to be derived from the objects known.

Now 'derived' here does not just mean 'causally derived' (though no doubt many if not most pieces of speculative knowledge must be causally derived from the objects known). It indicates, rather, a

[10] Donellan (alone?) sees this; see *J. Phil* 1963.

formal priority or onus of match. The putative knowledge must match its object in order to be knowledge. Suppose I am intentionally painting the wall yellow and you have an observational belief that I am so doing. Then your belief is knowledge because I am so doing or, in older terminology, that I am so doing is the (formal) cause of your knowledge.

But, Anscombe maintains, in practical knowledge the onus of match is the other way round. Practical knowledge is 'the cause of what it understands'. As with 'derive' above, 'the cause' here does not just mean 'the efficient cause' or a causally sufficient and/or necessary condition. It indicates a formal priority. The intentional action must match the knowledge in order to be that action. Suppose I am intentionally painting the wall yellow. Then my knowledge of what I am doing makes it to be the case that that is so. I am so doing because (in virtue of the fact that) I know it.

It will be said – but what if I'm not painting the wall yellow but, being colour-blind, only think I am? Well, in that case of course I am in error. But it was never claimed that the agent's knowledge of his intentional actions was infallible. On the contrary, Anscombe believes that where there is no possibility of error we should not speak of knowledge but only in terms of 'can say'. But when I am in error, the mistake lies in the performance, not in a judgment about what I am doing. (Contrast again your speculative knowledge. If you, being colour-blind, think I am painting the wall yellow when I am not, the mistake lies in your judgment about what I am doing.)

It is important to note that it is its being non-speculative which makes the agent's knowledge non-observational. It is *not* non-observational in virtue of how it feels to the agent – that I know 'straight off' or 'directly' or 'have a special awareness of' what I am doing, in a way (perhaps) similar to the way in which I know the position of my limbs. Maybe the knowledge does feel the same, but it wouldn't matter if it didn't. For my knowledge of, e.g., the position of my limbs is still speculative, i.e., derived from (determined as knowledge by) the position of my limbs and hence the fact that it is non-observational is incidental. It might not have been. But practical knowledge, not being derived from the object known, *could not possibly* be observational.

Now it might be thought that in making practical knowledge non-speculative Anscombe has rendered it miraculous. After all, the knowledge that I have of the position of my limbs, and of the past through memory, is non-observational but the fact that it is (causally) derived from the objects known explains why it is not miraculous. If I had non-observational knowledge of the position of your limbs or of past events with which I had no connection that would

Rosalind Hursthouse

be miraculous precisely because it would not be causally connected with its object.[11] But as I noted in the footnote qualifying the meaning of 'non-observational' (n. 9), Anscombe's account does not involve denying that observation is relevant. She says that practical knowledge involves 'knowing one's way about' the matters involved in the intentional action in question (§48), and what this amounts to is that I have certain observational capacities and lack others, have learnt to do certain things and not others. So, for instance, I can't see what is happening behind me, and hence cannot, without special practice, make the shadow of my hands do a little dance behind me without looking. So if I said, waving my hands, that I was making their shadow do a little dance behind me, and was, and could regularly do this, so my claims counted as knowledge and not coincidence, *that* would be miraculous.

We should note what sense, on this account, is to be given to the claim that the agent's knowledge is special 'in virtue of being non-observational'. The specialness of the agent's knowledge does not lie in some special access that he has to some special object, say his intention. Rather, it is conceptually guaranteed by the nature of intentional action itself. An intentional action essentially is that which is determined by the agent's knowledge (not merely that *of which* the agent has special knowledge, for that would still be speculative). And since agent's knowledge could not make it to be the case that the action had certain causes, the intentional action could not essentially be an action with this further feature.

It is also noteworthy how readily Anscombe's account of my knowledge of my present intentional action extends to cover my knowledge of my future intentional actions where this manifests itself in expressions of intention which are not (merely) predictions. On any speculative causalist account my knowledge of my future actions must be derived from something present. How then to distinguish expression of intention from mere prediction? But on Anscombe's account, an expression of intention is that, and not merely a prediction, because of the agent's knowledge. With a prediction, the onus of match is on what is said; if I don't do what you predicted I would do, the mistake lies in your judgment. But if I don't do what I said I was going to do when I expressed my intention, I did not make an error in judgment, there was no fact about which I was mistaken, but error in performance. (Or I changed my mind.) And here too my observational and other capacities – my knowing my way about – are all that is needed to guarantee that my knowledge is not miraculous. If I regularly announced my intentions to meet people in the street without having arranged it, or to

[11] Cf. Pears, *Questions in the Philosophy of Mind*, p. 9.

catch buses running outside the timetable, or to shoot arrows over the house and hit my brother and did so, *that* would be miraculous. But no special causal connection with something present is needed to explain why my knowledge that I'm going to the opera tomorrow is not miraculous.

But on the causalist view, an agent's knowledge-of-his-present-or-future-intentional-action *must* be speculative knowledge of action-caused-by-certain-mental-items. Only on something like Anscombe's view of intentional action can one reap the benefits of making practical knowledge genuinely non-speculative.

I mentioned at the outset one beauty of Anscombe's account of intention; I conclude by mentioning another. In this post-Cartesian age, we are still looking for a satisfactory account of first person knowledge. I know a lot of things about myself – what I'm intending or trying to do, what I'm going to do (intend to do), that I believe that such and such, want to do so and so, remember hearing such and such, hope to do so and so, seem to see such and such ... and I know all these things in a way that no-one else does or could. On any Cartesian or neo-Cartesian picture it will be natural to give a uniform account of this self-knowledge, in terms of my knowledge of how things are with me 'considered by myself'. It is the beauty of Anscombe's description of practical knowledge that, entirely abandoning this picture, it makes my so-called *self*-knowledge of my intention in acting extend beyond my head into the world, without undercutting its essentially first person nature. Although, of course, there is nothing in her to suggest that a general, uniform, account of self-knowledge should or could be given, she shows us the possibility of giving a non-Cartesian account of each of the other cases.[12]

Postscript
I wrote this paper in the early eighties. Reading it now, I still stand by everything I said in it. The fact that I could extend my list of stalking horses in n.2 (which does look a little dated), serves only to reinforce my willingness to underwrite, now, my original claim that '*present* fashion has taken the wrong path'.

[12] Evans had begun this. See *The Varieties of Reference*, 7.4.

Does moral subjectivism rest on a mistake?

PHILIPPA FOOT

I have asked that this article should be reprinted in the volume dedicated to Elizabeth Anscombe because it in particular reflects throughout my great indebtedness to her. I remember, as long ago as the late 1940s confidently referring to 'the difference between descriptive and evaluative reasoning' in one of the many discussions that we began to have from that time on. She, genuinely puzzled, simply asked, 'What do you mean?'

The paper is a revised text of the Hart Lecture delivered in Oxford University on 10 May 1994. Many thanks for help from Rosalind Hursthouse, Gavin Lawrence and, most especially, Michael Thompson to whose work I am greatly indebted.

This paper is about the moral subjectivism that, for the last sixty years or so, has dominated moral philosophy in England, America, and other countries in which analytic philosophy is taught. This is the subjectivism – often called 'noncognitivism' – that came to the fore with A. J. Ayer, C. L. Stevenson and Richard Hare, informed the work of John Mackie and many others, and has lately appeared, refreshed, in Allan Gibbard's 'expressivist' account of 'normative' language.[1] Simon Blackburn, reviewing Gibbard's *Wise Choices, Apt Feelings*, has said that he hopes this book will set the agenda for moral philosophy for the next fifty years. I myself, for all my admiration for Gibbard, hope that it will not do that. So I should say why

---

[1] A. J. Ayer, *Language, Truth and Logic* (London: Gollancz, 1936); C. L. Stevenson, *Ethics and Language* (New Haven: Yale University Press, 1945); R. M. Hare, *The Language of Morals* (Oxford: Clarendon Press, 1965); J. L. Mackie, *Ethics: Inventing Right and Wrong* (Harmondsworth: Penguin, 1977); A. Gibbard, *Wise Choices, Apt Feelings* (Cambridge, MA: Harvard University Press, 1990). I should mention here that although he has not abandoned his attack on what he calls 'Descriptivism' Hare does not want to be called either a subjectivist or a noncognitivist. See R. M. Hare, 'Objective Prescriptions', in A. P. Griffiths (ed.) *Ethics*, Royal Institute of Philosophy Lectures 1993 (Cambridge University Press, 1994). Also, R. M. Hare, 'Off on the Wrong Foot', *Canadian Journal of Philosophy*, Supp. Vol. 21.

Philippa Foot

I believe that these non-cognitivist theories – one and all – are based on a mistake.

To identify the common characteristic of the apparently somewhat diverse moral philosophies that I have just grouped together, and also to do justice to them, it will be good to start by asking how the whole non-cognitivist business began. One finds its deepest roots in Hume. But more immediately, Ayer and Stevenson's emotivism, like Hare's prescriptivism, came into being as a result of 'the linguistic turn', popularised by logical positivism but developing far beyond it. For with 'linguistic philosophy' came the idea of explaining the singularity of moral judgment in terms of a special use of language, called 'evaluation' but more akin to exclamation and command than to anything one would normally mean by that term. With this idea, it seemed possible, at last, to say clearly what G. E. Moore had meant, or should have meant, when he insisted that goodness was a special kind of 'non-natural' property.[2] In the development of emotivism and prescriptivism the idea of a special ('non-natural') property was replaced by that of a special and essentially practical use of language. And this, it seemed, was a great discovery. The language of evaluation was 'emotive'. It expressed a speaker's feelings and attitudes, as well as inducing similar feelings and attitudes in others. Those who had these 'attitudes' 'favoured' the things they called 'good': the idea of an attitude being linked to a tendency to act. Such also was the doctrine of A. J. Ayer; and a little later R. M. Hare tied 'evaluation' even more closely to individual action, in his theory of universalised imperatives by which a speaker exhorted others and, in the acceptance of a first person imperative, committed himself to choose what he called 'good'. So 'prescriptivism' – a distinctive version of the doctrine that I have in my sights – was added to the emotivism with which it had started out. In an explicit definition of the 'prescriptive' use of language Hare wrote

> We say something prescriptive if and only if, for some act A, some situation S and some person P, if P were to assent (orally) to what we say, and not, in S, do A, he logically must be assenting insincerely.[3]

I shall come back to this definition later on. But first, something more general about the theories I am attacking. It is characteristic of those I have mentioned, and others inspired by them, to suggest that the making of any sincere moral judgment requires the

[2] G. E. Moore, *Principia Ethica* (Cambridge University Press, 1903).
[3] R. M. Hare, *Moral Thinking* (Oxford: Clarendon Press, 1981), p. 21.

presence of individual feeling, attitude, or intention, and thus goes beyond 'description' or 'assertion of fact'. It was recognised, of course, that the language contains many terms like 'courage' or 'justice' designed for description *as well* as moral judgment, but it was said that their 'descriptive' content could not reach all the way to moral evaluation, the speaker's feelings or commitments to action having to be added if that were to be on the scene. Hence the apparently unquestionable distinction between 'descriptive' and 'evaluative' language, more or less taken for granted in much of contemporary ethics.

In early versions of these theories it was suggested that only a demand for consistency set any limits on the classes of actions to which words such as 'morally good' or 'morally bad' could be applied. So the extra feature supposedly involved in moral judgment could stand on its own, ready to form the core of alien moral systems confronting, or even directly contradicting, our own, and if no linguistic device existed for expressing 'moral approval' or 'moral disapproval' in their purity, this was held to be merely an accident of language. Thus, these early theories were radically subjectivist, allowing the possibility even of bizarre so-called 'moral judgments' about the wrongness of running around trees right handed or looking at hedgehogs in the light of the moon, and thus opening up limitless possibilities of irresolvable moral conflict. Nowadays it is commonly admitted, I believe, that there is some content restriction on what can intelligibly be said to be a system of morality. Moreover, Hare himself has suggested that a fairly tight form of utilitarianism can actually be obtained from universalised prescriptivism.[4] So it is not the old battle against a 'free for all' subjectivism that I want to fight. The mistake that I referred to in my title is one I claim to find in the later, as in the earlier, versions of noncognitivism. Even if the very tightest limitations on 'descriptive content' were accepted – even Bentham's suggestion that when used in conjunction with the greatest happiness principle, words such as 'ought' and 'right' have meaning and otherwise not – 'description' would still not, according to these theories, reach all the way to moral judgment. Someone convinced of the utility – or whatever – of certain kinds of action would not – indeed could not – straightforwardly and with sincerity make the judgment about their moral goodness unless he found in himself the right feelings and attitudes, or was ready to take the step of committing himself to act in a particular way. For moral evaluation, something 'conative' had to be present as well as belief in matters of fact.

[4] See R. M. Hare, *Freedom and Reason* (Oxford: Clarendon Press, 1963).

Philippa Foot

What all these theories try to do, then, is to give the *conditions of use* of sentences such as 'It is morally objectionable to break promises', in terms of something that must be true about the speaker. He must have certain feelings or attitudes; he must commit himself to acting in a certain way; he must at least feel remorse if he does not so act. *Meaning was thus to be explained in terms of a speaker's attitude, intentions, or state of mind.* And this opened up a gap between moral judgments and assertions, with the idea that truth conditions give, and may exhaust, the meaning of the latter but not the former. Thus it seemed that *fact*, complementary to assertion, had been distinguished from *value*, complementary to the expression of feeling, attitude or commitment to action. Propositions about matters of fact were assertible if their truth conditions were fulfilled, but moral judgments, through conditions of utterance, were essentially linked to an individual speaker's subjective state.

It is this kind of thing that seems to me all wrong. That is what I intended in suggesting that moral subjectivism 'rests on a mistake'. So what, then, is the mistake? It is the mistake of so construing what is 'special' about moral judgment that the grounds of a moral judgment do not reach all the way to it. Whatever 'grounds' may have been given, someone may be unready, indeed unable, to make the moral judgment, because he has not *got* the attitude or feeling, is not *in* the 'conative' state of mind, is not *ready* to take the decision to act: whatever it is that the theory says is required. It is this gap between ground and moral judgment that I am denying. In my view there are no such conditions on moral judgment and therefore no such gap.

It was not, however, a fit of collective madness that seized moral philosophers in the thirties, and still grips them today. Their theories were devised to take account of something that really is a feature of moral judgment: the 'action guiding' character of morality, which Hume had insisted on and taken as the foundation of his moral philosophy. Morality, Hume had said, is necessarily practical, serving to produce and prevent action, and I shall call this 'Hume's practicality requirement'.[5] Nor am I denying that his demand must be met. My contention is rather that the theories I am attacking tried to meet it in the wrong way. This, substantially, is what this paper is about.

If I am to prove my thesis I must, of course, produce an alternative to the noncognitivist way of showing that moral judgment is essentially 'action guiding'. So what is my own account of the matter? It is, to state it briefly, that Hume's demand is met by the (most un-Humean) thought that acting morally is part of practical rationality.

[5] See David Hume, *A Treatise of Human Nature*, Book III, part 2.

110

Does moral subjectivism rest on a mistake?

Now I am quite aware that to make this suggestion will seem most foolhardy: a case of putting one's head, philosophically speaking, into the lion's mouth. For is it not difficult to establish even coincidence between moral and rational action? What, after all, about those problem cases where justice or charity forbids the only way out of a tight corner, and the life of the agent may even be at stake? Isn't the demonstration of the rationality of just action a problem with which David Gauthier, for instance, has been wrestling for years, with great energy and skill?[6] And isn't this the fence at which I myself have repeatedly fallen, trying now this way now that of getting over – from 'Moral Beliefs' in 1958 to 'Morality as a System of Hypothetical Imperatives' in 1972?[7] All of this is true, and if I am hopeful of greater success this time round it is because I think I now see why I couldn't have managed it before. Roughly speaking it was because I still held a more or less Humean theory of reasons for action, taking it for granted that reasons had to be based on an agent's desires. To be sure, in another article 'Reasons for Action and Desires', *Aristolelian Society, Supplementary Vol.*, 1972, I had (rather inconsistently with my doubts about the rational status of morals) allowed considerations of self-interest an independent 'reason-giving' force. But this didn't help with the rationality of disinterested justice, which rationality I was, rather scandalously, inclined to restrict to those whose desires were such as to allow them to be described as lovers of justice. I have therefore, rightly, been accused by my critics of reintroducing subjectivity at the level of rationality while insisting on objectivity in the criteria of moral right and wrong.

In common with others, I took it for granted at that time that a discussion of the rationality of moral action would start from some theory or other about what reasons for action must be: rather favouring a desire-fulfilment theory, with some special allowance for the force of considerations of self-interest. I now believe that both the self-interest theory of rationality, and the theory of rationality as desire fulfilment are mistaken. Moreover there seems to be a mistake of *strategy* involved in trying to fit the rationality of moral action into either theory; such an enterprise implying that we first come to a theory of rational action, and then try as best we can to slot in the rationality of acts of justice and charity.

That this was a mistake of strategy was suggested to me by my

[6] See D. Gauthier, *Morals by Agreement* (Oxford: Clarendon Press, 1986).

[7] P. R. Foot, 'Moral Beliefs', Proceedings of the Aristotelian Society, vol. 59 (1958–9) and 'Morality as a System of Hypothetical Imperatives', *The Philosophical Review*, vol. 89, no. 3, July 1972.

Philippa Foot

friend the late Warren Quinn, and while I do not think that he really developed the idea himself, the same thought is implicit in his attack on end-neutral, Humean, theories of rationality, in an important article 'Putting Rationality in its Place' that has just been reprinted in the collection of his papers called *Morality and Action*, following his very sadly early death.[8] What, asked Quinn, would be *so important* about practical rationality if it were rational to seek to fulfil any, even a despicable, desire? In asking this he was questioning whether it is right to think that moral action has to be brought under a pre-established concept of practical rationality, and this seems to me to be very important indeed. My own view is, and perhaps his was, that there is no question here of 'fitting in' *in either direction*. I do not, therefore, want to canvas the rival claims of self-interest or maximum satisfaction of desires as accounts of practical rationality, and then try, as Gauthier and many others do, to explain the rationality of moral actions in terms of the one that wins out. But nor do I think, on the other side, that the whole of practical rationality can be brought under the umbrella of 'morality', as we usually understand that term.

As I see it, the rationality of, say, telling the truth, keeping promises, or helping a neighbour, is *on a par* with the rationality of self-preserving action, and of the careful and cognisant pursuit of other innocent ends; each being a part or aspect of practical rationality. The different considerations are on a par, moreover, in that a judgment about what is required by practical rationality must take account of their interaction: of the weight of the ones we call non-moral as well as those we call moral. For it is not always rational to give help where it is needed, to keep a promise, or even, I believe, absolutely always to speak the truth. If it is to be said that 'moral considerations' are always 'overriding' it cannot be *these* considerations that we refer to, but must rather be the overall 'moral judgment' about what, in all the circumstances, should be done. Sorting out this particular point of precedence is, I think, a matter of keeping one's head and remembering that some expressions do and some do not imply overall judgment: imprudence, for instance, being by definition contrary to rationality, but self-sacrifice not. Leaving aside this complication, we may think of the different requirements of rationality in action as on a par. And I shall argue later that there is a unity to these different grounds of practical rationality that may not be obvious right away.

Before coming to that, however, I have to argue that just and

[8] W. S. Quinn, *Morality and Action*, (Cambridge University Press, 1994).

112

charitable actions are indeed requirements of practical rationality. How can I now find a way of showing that reason may demand that promises be kept, truth told, or succour given, even when that is contrary to self-interest or to heart's desire?

The demonstration should start, I believe, with some observations on the nature of a moral virtue. It is in the concept of a moral virtue that in so far as someone possesses it his actions are good; which is to say that he acts well. Moral virtues bring it about that one who has them acts well, and we must enquire as to what this does and does not mean.

What, for instance, distinguishes a just person from one who is unjust? The fact that he keeps his contracts? That cannot be right, because circumstances may make it impossible for him to do so. Nor is it that he saves life rather than kills innocent people, for by blameless mishap he may kill rather than save. 'Of course,' someone will say at this point, 'it is the just person's intention not what he actually brings about that counts'. But why not say, then, that it is the distinguishing characteristic of the just that *for them certain considerations count as reasons for action*? (And as reasons of a certain weight.) And will it not be the same with other virtues, as for instance the virtues of charity, courage, and temperance? Those who possess these virtues possess them in so far as they recognise certain considerations (such as the fact of a promise, or of a neighbour's need) as powerful, and in many circumstances compelling, reasons for acting. They recognise the reasons, and act on them.

Thus the description 'just', as applied to a man or woman, speaks of how it is with them in respect of the acceptance of a certain group of considerations as reasons for action. If justice is a virtue, this is what the virtue of justice rectifies, i.e. makes good. It is no part of moral goodness — which is goodness of character — that someone should be physically strong, should move well, or talk well, or see well. But he must act well, in a sense that is given primarily at least by his recognition of the force of particular considerations as reasons for acting: that and the influence that this has on what he does. The just person aims at keeping his promises, paying what he owes, and defending those whose rights are being violated, so far as such actions are required by the virtue of justice. Likewise, he recognises certain limitations on what he may do even for some virtue-given end; as he may not kill an innocent person even for the sake of stopping someone else from killing a greater number, though he may, as Elizabeth Anscombe has remarked, destroy someone's property to stop the spread of a fire. And again he acts accordingly. Similarly, if charity is a virtue, this is because it makes its possessor's action good in the area of aims such as the relief of poverty. Here again, recognising particular considerations as reasons for action, he acts on these reasons as he should.

Now in describing moral virtues in terms of a) the recognition of particular considerations as reasons for acting, and b) the relevant action, I have only been expressing very familiar and time-honoured ideas of moral goodness. But how can it be denied that I have at the same time been talking about practical rationality? The discussion has been about human goodness in respect of reason-recognition and reason-following, and if this is not practical rationality I should like to know what is! The reply from those who hold a pre-conceived theory of practical rationality will be, no doubt, that rationality is the following of perceived self-interest; alternatively that it is the pursuit, careful and cognisant, of the maximum satisfaction of present desires: each respondent suggesting that one of these rival theories gives *the* concept of practical rationality. At the very least, they may argue, such theories give a *different* idea of practical rationality, to set beside the one that emerged from our discussion of justice and charity as virtues having to do with the following of reasons. But I suggested earlier that this was a mistake: that we should not think in terms of rival theories, but of the different parts of practical rationality, no one of which should be mistaken for the whole. An action can be contrary to practical rationality in that it is dishonest or disrespectful of others' rights, *or* that it is foolishly imprudent; *or*, again, that the agent is e.g., careless, timid, or half-hearted in going for what he wants.

Given that there are at least so many different cases, which it may or may not be useful to categorise, it is not surprising that the blanket term 'practical irrationality', and cognates such as 'contrary to practical reason', may go along with different subsidiary descriptions. I do not want to argue about bits of linguistic usage: about where, for instance, the particular term 'irrational', or again 'unreasonable', is or isn't at home. It is obvious that some terms such as 'silly' or 'foolish', and perhaps also 'irrational', do not correctly describe the actions of, for instance, the Great Train Robbers; even though in being dishonest, and careless of the life of the train driver, what they did was contrary to justice, and so to practical rationality. It makes for nothing but confusion to centre an argument about practical reason around one particular expression cut off from its genuine application, as Allan Gibbard does in supposing moral judgment to be expressible in terms of what does or does not 'make sense'. As if *that* were the way to say what was wrong with the train robbers' actions, or with the notorious landlord Rachmann's dealings with his tenants!

There is no doubt but that there are different kinds of cases of contrary-to-reasonness, and not surprisingly it is possible to contravene rationality in more than one way at the same time. I once read of a burglar who was caught because he sat down to watch television in the house he was burgling, thus adding the contrary-to-reasonness of imprudence to that of dishonesty. Because his actions were faulty in that he did not hurry away with the swag, we can say, if we like, that he *should* have done so. It does not follow, however, that he would have acted well if he had avoided imprudence, because it is not possible to act with full practical rationality in the pursuit of a bad end.

It is, I think, possible to see, even if not as yet very clearly, the common thread linking these different parts of practical rationality. The root notion is that of the goodness of human beings in respect of their actions; which means, to repeat, goodness of the will rather than of such things as sight or dexterity, concentration or memory. Kant was perfectly right in saying that moral goodness was goodness of the will; the idea of practical rationality is throughout a concept of this kind. He seems to have gone wrong, however, in thinking that an abstract idea of practical reason applicable to rational beings as such could take us all the way to anything like our own moral code. For the evaluation of human action depends also on essential features of specifically human life.

Elizabeth Anscombe brings out this dependence of morality on the life of our species in a passage in her article 'Promising and its Justice'. There she points out facts about human life that make it necessary for human beings to be able to bind each other to action through institutions such as promising. (There are so few other ways in which one person can reliably get another to do what he wants. And what hangs on this may, we might add, be something very important, such as that his children should be cared for after his death.)

Anscombe writes:

[G]etting one another to do things without the application of physical force is a necessity for human life, and that far beyond what could be secured by ... other means.

[Such a procedure is] ... an instrument whose use is part and parcel of an enormous amount of human activity and hence of human good; of the supplying both of human needs and of human wants so far as the satisfactions of these are compossible ... It is scarcely possible to live in a society without encountering it and even being involved in it.[9]

[9] G. E. M. Anscombe, *Collected Philosophical Papers* (Oxford: Basil Blackwell, 1981), vol. III, 18.

Philippa Foot

Anscombe is pointing here to what she has elsewhere called an 'Aristotelian necessity': that which is necessary because and in so far as good hangs on it.[10] We invoke the same idea when we say that it is necessary for plants to have water, for birds to build nests, for wolves to hunt in packs, and for lionesses to teach their cubs to kill. These 'Aristotelian necessities' depend on what the particular species of plants and animals need, on their natural habitat, and the ways of making out that are in their repertoire. These things together determine what it is for members of a particular species to be as they should be, and to do that which they should do.[11] And for all the enormous differences between the life of humans and that of plants or animals, we can see that human defects and excellences are similarly related to what human beings are and what they do. We do not need to be able to dive like gannets, nor to see in the dark like owls; but our memory and concentration must be such as to allow us to learn language, and our sight such that we can recognise faces at a glance; while like lionesses human parents are defective if they do not teach their young the skills that they need to survive. Moreover, in that we are social animals, we depend on each other as do wolves that hunt in packs, with co-operation such as our own depending on special factors such as conventional arrangements. Like the animals we do things that will benefit others rather than ourselves: there is no good case for assessing the goodness of human action by reference only to good that each person brings to himself. Is it, one wonders, some lingering shadow of the thoroughly discredited doctrine of psychological egoism – of the belief that all *human* action is directed to the good of the agent himself – that inclines us to an egoistic concept of practical rationality? I do not know what else should make us think that the evaluation of reason-following behaviour must be altogether different in its conceptual structure from the evaulation of the behaviour of an animal. And it will surely not be denied that there is something wrong with a free-riding wolf, who eats but does not take part in the hunt, as with a member of the species of dancing bees who finds a source of nectar but does not let other bees know where it is. These 'free-riding' individuals of a species whose members work together are just as *defective* as those who have defective hearing, sight, or powers of locomotion.

[10] Ibid., 15, 18–19, 100–1, 139.

[11] I have written here of species, but it might be better to use the words 'life form' as Michael Thompson does. See his article 'The Representation of Life' in R. Hursthouse, G. Lawrence and W. S. Quinn (eds) *Virtues and Reasons* (Oxford University Press, 1995). Here I am particularly indebted to his work.

Does moral subjectivism rest on a mistake?

I am therefore, quite seriously, likening the basis of moral evaluation to that of the evaluation of behaviour in animals. I would stress, however, that it is important not to underestimate the degree to which human communication and reasoning changes the scene. The goods that hang on human co-operation, and hang too on such things as respect for truth, art and scholarship, are much more diverse, and much harder to delineate than are animal *goods*. Animals are different also from us in that to do what they should do – what is needed and is within their capacity – they do not have to understand what is going on; whereas a human being can and should understand that, and why, there is reason for, say, keeping a promise, or behaving fairly. This last may seem a tall order, but this human understanding is not anything hard to come by. We all know enough to say 'How could we get on without justice?', 'Where would we be if no one helped anyone else?' or 'How could we manage if there were no way of making decisions for us all?'

Anyone who thinks about it can see that for human beings the teaching and following of morality is something necessary. We can't get on without it. And this is the nub of the proper answer to the challenge that I made in 'Morality as a System of Hypothetical Imperatives', where I asked why it should be thought rational to follow morality, but not to obey duelling rules or silly rules of etiquette. In that article I myself made a rotten job of answering my own question because, still under the influence of Humean ideas of practical rationality, I thought irrelevant what is now turning out to be most relevant. (It was, I remember, a remark of Rosalind Hursthouse's that put me right about this.)

Later on, Warren Quinn helped me by pointing out that after this change I could at least claim to have found the basis for a unified theory of rationality. For if moral values are an 'Aristotelian necessity' for human beings so too is a reasonable modicum of self-interest. Once grown, we can look out for ourselves much better than anyone else can do it for us.[12] Good hangs, too, on the careful and cognisant pursuit of many more particular ends.

It is time now for me to return to the main line of my argument against noncognitivism. It is because I see practical rationality as determined in this way that I claim to be able to interpret the 'action-guidingness' of moral judgment in terms of the practical

[12] In theory, this could, of course, be different for some other kinds of rational beings. Perhaps they would find it impossible to think calmly about *their own* future, and would have invented a kind of 'buddy system' by which each person had someone else to look out for him. We should find this extremely inconvenient except in bringing up children when they are small.

Philippa Foot

rationality of moral action. And please notice that I have not reintroduced, via the concept of practical rationality itself, a subjective (agent-centred) condition on moral judgment. For I have not subscribed to a desire-based, Humean, theory of practical rationality: nor have I any reason to go along with Gibbard's 'expressivist' account of what it is we are doing when we say that certain action is rational. Nothing of that kind has had any part in what I have said.

If I am right, therefore, about judgments of practical rationality and their ground, and right in seeing the kind of thing that Elizabeth Anscombe said about promising as simply one particular application of general (*species-based*) criteria of evaluation, I can claim to see how, in principle, a non-subjectivist – indeed cognitivist – reply might be given to Hume's demand that morality be shown to be 'necessarily practical'. Considerations about such things as promising, neighbourliness and help for those in trouble, have, I maintain, the same kind of connection with action as do considerations of self-interest or of means to our ends: the connection going in each case through the concept of practical rationality and the facts of human life. So I think that we can see as hopeful the project of producing a cognitivist alternative to theories such as emotivism, prescriptivism and expressivism: an alternative that takes care of just what they were trying to take care of, in the way of a necessary connection between moral judgment and action.

I am sure that it will be objected at this point that even if, along these lines, a certain conceptual link has been shown to hold between moral language and action, via the fact that a moral judgment speaks of what there is reason to do, this will not have put the connection in the right place. For, it will be said, a relation has not been shown that holds between moral judgment and the action of *each and every individual*. This, however, I would dispute. On a 'practical rationality' account, a moral judgment says something about the action of any individual to whom it applies; namely something about the reason that there is for *him* to do it or not do it; whether or not he recognises that, and whether or not, if he does recognise it, he also acts on it as he should. Moreover, it can explain moral action in an individual who knows that he has reason to act morally; because acting on reasons is a basic mode of operation in human beings. This too is part of my account of the way in which morality is necessarily practical: it serves to produce and prevent action, *because the understanding of reasons can do that*.

We must be careful, however, not to tie moral judgment too closely to action. One who is the subject of a true moral judgment does not always do what it says he should do, since he may not recognise its truth, and may not act on it even if he does. In spite of recognising the force of Hume's 'practicality requirement' we must allow for ignorance, for weakness of will, and also for the phenomenon of shamelessness. It should be seen as an advantage, not a disadvantage, if the 'rationality' account leaves room for this last. No doubt quite open shamelessness is fairly rare (even in our time) at least in the circles in which most philosophers live. But it is important to recognise that shamelessness can co-exist with the use of moral language, and to see that this shamelessness is not the same as insincerity. I have read, for instance, of a member of a group of city louts out for a day in the country to hunt down some small inoffensive animal, who, though described as 'the conscience of the group', said: 'I know I'm on earth 70 years and that I'm not going anywhere else. If I choose to spend my day out in the countryside doing whatever I feel like then that's what I'll do'. And again of a certain Brooklyn machine politician who had the gall to say that while people think it hard to stand up for what is right, what is really hard is what he was doing, 'standing up day after day, week after week, for what is wrong'. Like Alec D'Urberville in Hardy's novel, this politician might have said 'I have lived bad, and I shall die bad', meaning what he said, but without the slightest intention to reform.

There are, it is true, some who try to hide their shamelessness by making an attack on morality. But more people than we like to admit are simply shameless. Do they then not 'endorse the norm' of justice and charity, to use Gibbard's words for what he sees as the 'state of mind' that is 'expressed' in moral judgment? Well I do not know what is meant by this somewhat contrived expression. I suppose that most criminals do not think much about the topic of morality, being in this rather like the British politician Alan Clark who, when confronted with a nasty fact about the arms trade, is reported to have said: 'I do not much fill my mind with what one set of foreigners do to another.' I suppose one can evade either 'endorsing' or not 'endorsing' morality, or part of morality, by simply refusing to think about it; and I suppose that most of us do that at times. But D'Urberville seems not, on the night he seduced Tess, to have pushed morality out of sight, when he said 'I have lived bad, and I shall die bad', and it is important to contrast his mentality with the point of view of those whom we may call '(ideological) immoralists', as e.g. Thrasymachus, Callicles, Nietzsche, or Gide. For the latter queried whether human goodness and badness are what they are supposed to be, whereas D'Urberville implicitly endorsed ordinary moral opinion, as did the Brooklyn machine politician, and perhaps also the 'city hunter' who seems to have thought that there was reason for him to let harmless animals live. By contrast with

Philippa Foot

these shameless individuals, the immoralists are bringing arguments in favour of some different standard of human goodness.[13]

I am not, of course, denying that there are many ambiguous
cases; but the two poles, of shamelessness and immoralism, nevertheless exist. And it is not the shameless but those who in their heart
of hearts agree with, say, Thrasymachus or Nietzsche who are
insincere if they speak as we do about what is right and wrong.

It follows, therefore, from the line of argument of this paper that
Hare – who said that moral language was 'prescriptive', and who so
defined the prescriptive use of language that anyone who assents to
a prescriptive proposition that in circumstances C an action A is
morally wrong, but nevertheless does A in C, is as a matter of logic
insincere – said something that is not true. Moral judgments, while
we may want to call them 'prescriptive' for some other reason, are
not 'prescriptive' *in this sense*. So no good reason has so far been
given for thinking that there is any kind of 'logical gap' between a
moral judgment and its grounds.

At this point, however, I must return to the subject of the 'practicality' of morality, to see how my account of it works out in face
of a rather different version of noncognitivism that is popular
today. I pointed out earlier that noncognitivism starts out from the
obviously correct idea that moral judgment has a special connection
with the actions which, as Hume said, it 'serves to produce and prevent'. Nor is this a contingent connection. It is in the concept of
morality that the thought that something ought to be done has a
relation to action lacked by such thoughts as that the earth is round,
or strawberries sweet, or many lives lost in wars. In this paper I
have accepted this premise but interpreted it differently, suggesting
that it is because moral action is a requirement of practical rationality that it has a special connection with the will. But it is just here
that some of my noncognitivist opponents will move in, scenting
victory. For they will insist that the fact of an agent's having reason
to do something (say to keep promises) is itself dependent on his
feelings, passions, or desires. And so, they will argue, if a moral
judgment about what I ought to do implies that I have reason so to
act, the judgment would seem to imply not just 'cognitions' but also
something 'conative': something having to do with an engagement
of the will. A noncognitivist, neo-Humean theory of reasons for
action is thus being called in to support a neo-Humean account of
moral judgment.

To many of its contemporary proponents this account of reasons
for action will probably seem particularly telling against an account

[13] And so, in Gavin Lawrence's graphic term we have *them* in our net.

of the practical aspect of morality such as the one I have given. For they too think of one who makes a moral judgment as necessarily having reason to act. A person's moral views suffice on occasion to explain his action: the moral judgment gave him a 'motivating reason' to do what he did. And this, my opponents believe, implies a fact about him: a fact about his attitudes, feelings or desires.

In the form in which this argument is now often put forward it begins, therefore, from the premise that moral judgments are 'motivating reasons' for action; by which it is meant that people do things simply because they think that they ought to do so. And this is followed by a particular account of what it is for anyone to have such a motivating, action-explaining, reason as part of his 'psychological state'.

The seduction of this account of reasons for action is considerable. It rests, no doubt, on what John McDowell has called the 'hydraulic' picture of the psychological determinants of action: a picture of desires as forces moving the will in certain directions, with action the result of a combination of belief and desire.[14] Such a picture is just as suspect as McDowell says it is; but what, we must ask, has ever given us such a picture? Where does *its* seduction lie?

To answer this question it will be useful to consider an article by Michael Smith in which what he calls 'the Humean theory of motivation' is defended. He writes

> ... the distinctive feature of a motivating reason to φ is that in virtue of having such a reason an agent is in a state that is *potentially explanatory* of his φing ... [And] it would seem to be part of our concept of what it is for an agent's reasons to have the potential to explain his behaviour that his having these reasons is a fact about him; that is, that the goals that such reasons embody are *his* goals.[15]

We are likely to be seduced by this because it is natural to think in the following way:

Take as an example that of someone who throws away his supply of cigarettes. He does so because he wants to give up smoking. And he wants to give up smoking because he wants a healthy old age. The series goes on – A for the sake of B – but it can't go on for ever.[16] And must it not end with something that the agent 'just wants'; in

[14] See J. McDowell, 'Are Moral Requirements Hypothetical Imperatives?', *The Aristotelian Society, Supplementary Volume*, 1978, 13–29.

[15] M. Smith, 'The Humean Theory of Motivation', *Mind*, NS XCVI, (1987) 38.

[16] Cp David Hume, *An Enquiry Concerning the Principles of Morals*, Appendix I.

other words with some 'conative' element in his individual psychological state?

The question is meant to be rhetorical; but the answer to it is 'No'. For what, we must ask, gives the agent this goal? Does he find himself trembling at the thought of cancer at fifty? Is he in a state of anxiety at the thought of how much he smokes? Perhaps. But nothing of this kind has to be part of the story, as Smith himself admits. So why do we say that what gets the whole thing going must be a desire or other 'conative' element in the subject's 'psychological state'? Suppose instead that it is the recognition that there is reason for him, as for anyone else, to look after his future so far as circumstances allow? Why should not this be where the series of questions 'why?' comes to an end? Those already in thrall to the 'hydraulic' picture of the workings of the mind will deny it. Others may, however, consider the question *why should we not take the recognition of a reason for acting as bringing the series to a close*? Recognition of a reason gives the rational person a goal; and this recognition is, according to the argument of the present paper, based on facts and concepts not on some prior attitude, feeling or goal. The only fact about the individual's state of mind that is required for the explanatory force of the proposition about the requirement of rationality is that he does not (for some bizarre reason) deny its truth. He only needs to know, like most adults, that it is silly to disregard one's own future without special reason to do so. No special explanation is needed of why men take reasonable care of their own future; an explanation is needed when they do not. Nor does human co-operation need a special explanation. Most people know that it is, for instance, unreasonable to take benefits and give nothing in return.

In denying the neo-Humean account of reasons for action in general it is, however, important to stress that there are some that do depend on what a particular person wants. If I want to see the Taj Mahal I have reason to buy a ticket to India as someone who detests all things Eastern does not. The imperative is, as Kant would say, hypothetical: if I no longer want to go the reason may well disappear. Another obvious example is that of someone who, feeling hungry and having no food in the house, goes down the road to buy something to eat. If he were not hungry he would not have this reason to go, and unless there were some other reason in the offing the facts about the food shop and the empty larder could not explain why he went to the shop.

My conclusion is, therefore, that neither directly (through conditions on sincere moral utterances) nor indirectly (through the thought that moral judgment can explain action) does the acceptance of

'Hume's practicality requirement' give any support to noncognitivism in ethics. Nor has any reason been given for the existence of a 'logical gap' between a moral judgment and its grounds. The premises of a moral argument give grounds for an assertion about what it is morally good – and therefore about what it is practically rational – to do. And for anything that has been shown to the contrary, these premises could even entail the conclusion, though I have certainly not argued that this is so. I have very little idea of how much 'play' there will in the end turn out to be in disagreements between moralities, and how many grey areas, and irreconcilable opinions we shall want to recognise. One can keep an open mind about that.

What then is to be said about the relation between 'fact' and 'value'? The thesis of this paper is that the grounding of a moral argument is ultimately in facts about human life – facts of the kind that Anscombe mentioned in talking about the good that hangs on the institution of promising, and of the kind that I spoke of in saying why it was a part of rationality for human beings to take special care each for his or her own future. In my view, therefore, a moral evaluation does not stand over against the statement of a matter of fact, but rather has to do with facts about a particular subject matter, as do evaluations of such things as sight and hearing in animals, and other aspects of their behaviour. Nobody would, I think, take it as other than a plain matter of fact that there is something wrong with the hearing of a gull that cannot distinguish the cry of its own chick, as with the sight of an owl that cannot see in the dark. Similarly, it is obvious that there are objective, factual evaluations of such things as human sight, hearing, memory, and concentration, based on the life-form of our own species. Why, then, does it seem so monstrous a suggestion that the evaluation of the human will should be determined by facts about the nature of human beings and the life of our own species? Undoubtedly the resistance has something to do with the thought that the goodness of good action has a special relation to choice. But as I have tried to show, this special relation is not what noncognitivists think it, but rather lies in the fact that moral action is rational action, and in the fact that human beings are creatures with the power to recognise reasons for action and to act on them.

Ethics and psychology

ROGER TEICHMANN

> ...it is not profitable for us at present to do moral philosophy; that should be laid aside at any rate until we have an adequate philosophy of psychology, in which we are conspicuously lacking.[1]

These words state one of the principal theses of Elizabeth Anscombe's 'Modern Moral Philosophy' (1958). Later in the article, the point is reiterated more specifically and with more force:

> is it not clear that there are several concepts that need investigating simply as part of the philosophy of psychology and – as I should recommend – *banishing ethics totally* from our minds? Namely – to begin with: 'action', 'intention', 'pleasure', 'wanting'. More will probably turn up if we start with these.[2]

The psychological concepts which Anscombe mentions are ones which she herself did much to elucidate, in ways which made it possible to get a clearer view of a variety of ethical notions. A good number of these notions clustered around the moral agent – his character, his actions, *mens rea*, and so on. In this paper I want to look at another family of ethical notions, and the psychological concepts they are connected with – some of the 'more' that 'will probably turn up'. Of these notions it is also possible to say: an adequate philosophy of psychology is essential for understanding them. But it seems to me wrong to think that the philosophy of psychology can be done quite antecedently to the ethics; we cannot do the philosophy of psychology having 'banished ethics totally from our minds'. For the ethical and the psychological are here so intimately connected that in doing the second one finds oneself doing the first. This phenomenon can indeed be detected in Anscombe's own philosophy of psychology: her remark about banishing ethics was perhaps simply an expression of the view that moral philosophers were, in 1958, *very* off-track.

Wittgenstein wrote:

> My attitude towards him is an attitude towards a soul. I am not of the *opinion* that he has a soul.[3]

[1] G. E. M. Anscombe, 'Modern Moral Philosophy', in *Ethics, Religion and Politics: Collected Philosophical Papers, Vol. III* (Blackwell, 1981), p. 26.

[2] Anscombe, ibid., p. 38.

[3] Wittgenstein, *Philosophical Investigations*, trans. G. E. M. Anscombe, 3rd edn (Blackwell, 1967), p. 178.

Roger Teichmann

Here and elsewhere his purpose was to point to the fact that the basis of many of our psychological concepts is to be found in the natural reactions and attitudes we have to one another – reactions of sympathy, disgust, and so on. We do not apply these psychological concepts on the basis of theories about our fellow beings, nor on the basis of anything straightforwardly observational. Still less do we manifest sympathy, disgust, etc. via such things. Of course it is 'through our senses' that we know of others and come to respond to them – but only an incorrect (empiricist) view of perception would lead one to infer that we must therefore be constructing a theory or using a checklist of observable features. The need to postulate subconscious such theories or checklists is a symptom of the empiricist view's weakness: our ability to see another as joyful, or as in pain, is in fact spontaneous and unmediated – though naturally it is 'causally mediated'.

It is not only psychological concepts that are like this. Many perceptual concepts are in the same boat – in particular, concepts of 'secondary qualities'. Human beings are so constituted as to agree by and large in their perceptual discriminations: we lump lemons with bananas, strawberries with cherries. It is on the back of these primitive reactions or capacities that concepts like 'yellow' and 'red' get introduced; and their purpose or utility is connected with ordinary human perception (rather than with the aims of mature science, say).

There is in fact a general point about foundations here. *Some* groups of concepts must get introduced into the language other than by definition in terms of, or connection with, other concepts.[4] In the case of such concepts, 'the beginning is the deed'.[5] And it is hardly surprising that many psychological concepts should belong to this category: some of the most important interactions for members of our gregarious species must be with our fellow human beings. That we are very highly sensitive to all sorts of facts about each others' appearance and behaviour (in the broadest sense) is obvious. Such sensitivities are the basis both of a variety of psychological and other concepts (pain, smiling, sleep, anger ...), and of a variety of emotions and attitudes (trust, resentment, sympathy...).

A concept may have its basis in a primitive response and yet develop in certain ways – the picture will usually be complicated. But further development will not leave the primitive response behind if the importance and purpose of the concept (for us)

[4] There is a deliberate ambiguity here, as between the origins of a concept and the teaching of it to a child.

[5] Cf. *On Certainty*, par. 402, where Wittgenstein quotes Goethe's 'Im Anfang war die Tat' (*Faust*).

derives, to any significant degree, from that response. It will be the contention of this paper that philosophical theories of the mind that do not take proper account of our natural responses to one another will go astray in the way one might predict: they will feed a wrong-headed ethical outlook.

A concept where the psychological and the ethical notoriously come together is that of a 'person'. It is also a concept much chewed over by philosophers; indeed, it is sometimes unclear to what extent the concept chewed over is a myth of philosophers' making. A myth can have its basis in reality, of course – but a discussion of the nature of persons will often be reminiscent of one about Saint Nicholas. 'Do you mean the historical bishop of Myra, or the friend of children and bearer of presents?' is a question that surely needs settling. The same goes for 'Do you mean "person" as it's actually used in English, or some technical term of philosophy?' To each question, the reply might come: 'But they are one and the same!', or 'The second is just a more detailed version of the first'. The reply would be naive in both cases.

If 'person' is used as a term of art, no objection can be made to any definition – though objection can certainly be made to the hijacking of a familiar word with a different meaning, especially if the meaning of the one is (alleged to be) close to that of the other. Perhaps we are asked to accept an account of 'person' as a sort of half-way house between a term of art and the English term: a 'rational reconstruction' of the ordinary concept. But something can only be rationally reconstructed if it needs, or is susceptible of, reconstructing. Since this last cannot be assumed of the ordinary concept, I will start by taking the ordinary concept to be what is at issue. It will turn out neither to allow of reconstruction nor to resemble many of the versions presented of it.

Locke was the first philosopher to give what he took to be criteria of 'personhood'. These criteria included thinking, self-consciousness (in the philosophical sense), and memory of one's past. The concept thus delineated he distinguished from that of *man*, or *human being*. And he went on to describe the case of a 'rational parrot', famously concluding that such a parrot would have to be counted a person.

A philosopher's attitude to real or imaginary cases such as that of the rational parrot will usually say a lot. Now in ordinary English, and indeed (I would hazard the guess) in the English of Locke's day, one would not be using words correctly if one said of a parrot, however rational, 'That person is clever', 'There's a person I know who ...', etc. (If you think that these would be correct uses of 'person', I think that just shows you have been doing philosophy too long.)

Well, maybe a rational parrot wouldn't be a person. Maybe Locke's criteria of personhood are inadequate – they have come under much fire on other counts, after all. And plenty of attempts to give the criteria of personhood have been made since Locke's initial stab. But it is notable that many such attempts share with Locke's the feature of ascribing personhood to (probably imaginary) non-humans – a rather *simpatico* Martian might be eligible, for instance. It may be that this is deemed an asset of the theory: it seems to betoken a certain liberality and tolerance of outlook. Of course, very few *actual* beings benefit from this liberal outlook. The actual beings whose status is put in question will tend to be certain human beings, such as the very old or very young, the handicapped, and so on. But this is by the bye (for the moment).

The question to ask is, once again, '*Would* we call such creatures persons?' This question is easier to answer than it looks, I think, for the reason that a lot of science fiction involving very clever aliens has actually been written. Try writing some yourself; would you be able to describe a scene in which 'several people were in the room: two Martians, a Klingon, and Captain Picard'? (I assume that 'people' is the plural of 'person'.) This would, at best, be sloppy English; or it might conceivably come from getting into the habit of seeing those creatures (the Martians, etc.) *as* people, just as one can see Snoopy the dog as a person, in a certain sense – or the pots and pans in 'The Sorcerer's Apprentice', for that matter.

It will be apparent that I take 'person' to be at least a very close cousin of 'human being'. Locke, I think, was wrong to drive a wedge between the two notions. I also think that 'person' belongs among those 'primitive' concepts mentioned on p. 126, which are not taught by explicit or implicit reference to any list of criteria.[6] A person is, roughly, a 'somebody'. If a child says, 'Somebody's at the door', this is the same as 'There's a person at the door'. What has the child learnt, in learning this concept? A lot of what it can do is not, properly speaking, learnt at all, but innate; a human child just *can* recognise other human beings, notice their facial expressions, smile with them, etc. It is the capacity to recognise other human beings (often from the slightest of evidence, one might say) that forms the basis of the concept of a person, a somebody. This is why the class of persons is the same as that of human beings. But in so far as 'human being' is a biological concept, involving various 'marks' (such as the inability to breed with non-humans), one might

---

[6] In this respect, I am of course in agreement with what Strawson said of the concept of a person in his book *Individuals*.

doubt that 'person' and 'human being' are *synonyms*. I am not sure whether 'human being' can in fact be said to be a concept in biology, though I suppose *'homo sapiens'* is: the point could be made as one about the necessary co-extension of the classes 'person' and *'homo sapiens'*. This class, by the way, may be vague, or blurred at the edges. Our natural inbuilt response to other human beings is probably not absolutely 'all or nothing'.[7]

In passing, we could note that where some distinction is entirely lacking from a number of languages, that is a sign that it may not be the deep thing it is taken for. Ancient Greek and modern Chinese are just two of the languages which would have to translate an English sentence containing 'person' using the same word as would translate 'man' or 'human being'. – Interestingly enough, in that section of the *Essay* in which Locke outlines his theory of persons and personal identity, we find him using the word 'consciousness' in a way that provoked a footnote in the French edition to the effect that French had no word which could do justice to that notion, as intended by Locke. 'Consciousness' has become another of the most chewed over concepts; and the same schizophrenia, as between ordinary English and technical vocabulary, besets that philosophical discussion.

In moral philosophy, we often find 'person' used to signify 'creature worthy of such-and-such type or degree of regard'. The programme of supplying criteria of personhood then reflects, not merely the general philosophical itch for analysis, but an 'agenda' concerning the treatment of other people and creatures. If what I have said about the primitive nature of the concept of a person is right, this agenda is almost bound to be ill-founded. It will not now be enough to say that 'person' is, after all, being used in a technical sense; for the natural responses which form the basis of the concept 'person' *also* form the basis of many ethical concepts, so that a list of criteria for 'worthiness of moral regard' is liable (in ignoring natural responses) to go wrong.

I suspect that there is a connection between the philosophical itch

---

[7] It is a very interesting question, but one to answer which would be beyond the scope of this article, whether the blurredness of the concept *'homo sapiens'* corresponds, as it were, to that of 'person'. After death, I suspect that it does: decomposition is a gradual process, and our hesitation in calling what is before us a (dead) member of a certain species will increase alongside our hesitation in calling it a dead person, in saying things like 'There lies King Olaf'. (Our reactions to a corpse are of course different from those to a living person, but they are still specifically human in nature.)

for analysis and the production of moral agendas of the sort we are considering. Giving a list of criteria for worthiness of regard seems eminently *rational*: we can, using it, *decide* whether something is worthy of regard. The promise of philosophical analysis in general is often of the same kind. The alternative to a list of criteria of personhood seems to be reliance on our emotions, which, as is well known, are 'merely subjective' and hence not rational.

Of course you do not need a checklist of criteria to use a concept objectively. Think of colour-concepts (to revert to an earlier example). And the idea that the emotions in question are 'merely subjective' should appear dubious once we reflect that sufficient agreement in response is what very often grounds objectivity; whether the response counts as 'emotional' will be beside the point.

The view that the analytical approach is the more rational frequently gets expressed when it has been asserted that human beings are of central ethical importance. 'Surely such a view is irrational?' it is said. 'What *grounds* can you give for putting human beings centre-stage?' The charge may then be brought of 'speciesism', which is thought to be akin to racism and sexism, two similarly 'irrational' viewpoints.

There is a sort of logical mistake in this line of thought which it is fairly easy to state. Unless literally everything is worthy of moral regard – stones, chairs, atoms, shadows … – we will have to distinguish *somehow* between 'in' and 'out'. If you give four criteria, this is no better in itself than giving one: the four will each be as open to question as the one. You can as well ask, 'Why is consciousness important?' as ask, 'Why is being human important?'. Reasons run out somewhere. The question must be: *Where* do they run out? And the answer is: where you would expect them to – at the level of our natural responses to one another. (This picture does not apply to *all* 'language-games', of course. But I think it fairly obviously applies to our moral thought and talk.)

The actual consequences, or concomitants, of the 'list' approach to personhood, or to 'moral worthiness', are pretty clear. In its nature, the approach is bound to throw doubt on the claims upon us of various human beings. There are differences among philosophers about what exactly goes into personhood; but the differences seem insignificant beside the general trend, which is to count as non-persons, or as less personish, those who are, roughly, most distant from the healthy, well-functioning adult. (The differences seem slight by comparison with the similarities: readers will be reminded of the third main thesis of 'Modern Moral Philosophy'.)[8] At least one

[8] E.g. Anscombe, ibid., p. 34.

prominent moral philosopher is in favour of the infanticide, in not uncommon circumstances, of healthy babies (e.g. unwanted orphans):

> In thinking about this matter we should put aside feelings based on the small, helpless and – sometimes – cute appearance of human infants... If we can put aside these emotionally moving but strictly irrelevant aspects of the killing of a baby we can see that the grounds for not killing persons do not apply to newborn infants... The difference between killing defective and normal infants lies not in any supposed right to life which the latter has and the former lacks [sic], but in other considerations about killing. Most obviously there is the difference which often exists in the attitudes of the parents.[9]

Of course it is unlikely that such views simply arise out of a wrong notion of the concept of a person. There are various causes and influences at work: utilitarianism, affluence (which has made personal encounters with sickness and death rarer), and, I suppose, atheism, to name but three. It should go without saying that these things need not all be bad, in themselves; but they may together have contributed to a soil in which certain philosophical or ideological plants would flourish. With utilitarianism, to be sure, the reasons for this are, as it were, internal – most forms of utilitarianism involve a faulty or over-simple philosophy of mind.[10]

Let us now turn to the natural reactions and attitudes of which I have been speaking. One thing to make clear from the start is that an attitude's being natural does not entail its being good. Xenophobia and bloodlust are perfectly natural, I suppose – though, like other natural attitudes (for want of a better word), they are encouraged in some cultures more than in others.

Which brings us to another point: there is no sharp line between what is natural and what is culturally determined, but that there is a real difference here is surely indubitable. The culture is unimaginable in which it is customary for parents to be indifferent to their children, or for pigs to be befriended just as people are. Moreover, a custom or practice always has a *point*, a purpose in people's lives.

[9] Peter Singer, *Practical Ethics*, 1st edn (Oxford University Press, 1979), pp. 123–4, 131–2. *Practical Ethics* is standardly used as a moral philosophy textbook.

[10] A fault of classical utilitarianism was its taking such psychological states as pleasure to be sensations, or like sensations. The 'sensation' model of psychological states is one that has been often and effectively argued against by Elizabeth Anscombe.

This purpose could not derive from further customs, about which the question of purpose would be raised again; it must derive from our needs and proclivities. Our nature is, no doubt, very flexible and various, but it is for all that nature, not culture.

'But if our nature is flexible', it may be objected, 'won't it be flexible under the influence of reason and reflection? How else indeed are we to distinguish good reactions, such as pity, from bad ones, such as xenophobia? In which case, could not a reasoning philosopher excogitate, for example, criteria of personhood that would trump our normal protective impulses towards new-born babies?' – To answer this, we need to look carefully at what does count as the modification of natural reactions under the influence of reason.

Let us turn, once again, to some remarks of Wittgenstein. At par. 282 of the *Investigations*, Wittgenstein mentions the example of a child playing with a doll and taking it to be in pain. It seems that, as Wittgenstein says, we have here a secondary use of the concept *pain*. What is slightly tricky is saying in what way this use is secondary or non-literal. Wittgenstein remarks, or rather implies, that it is hard to imagine people ascribing pain *only* to inanimate things such as dolls. But one might also say that it is hard to imagine people ascribing pain *only* to non-human animals such as dogs. If this shows that 'That dog is in pain' involves a secondary use of the concept *pain*, still such a use is surely literal – whereas a doll cannot literally be in pain.

Is the child's taking her doll to be in pain like her taking an armchair to be a castle? Is it a case of pretending? – Even pretend-games can be taken seriously, of course. An imaginative child may to some extent 'live in an imaginary world': she may get upset or annoyed if one moves the castle-armchair from its proper position, say. But the possibility of getting upset *on behalf of* a doll, or of objecting if the doll is put in the wash, seems to be rather more than the possibility of a vivid pretend-game. Mightn't a small child's being upset on behalf of a doll be akin to her being upset on behalf of a pet hamster?

If a child gets too upset about her doll being put in the wash, an adult will be able to say: 'It's only a doll, and dolls don't feel pain.' But how is this possible, if the basis of ascriptions of pain is natural feelings of just the sort which the child is manifesting towards her doll?

It seems significant that this example has to do with a child. An adult who showed an undue attachment to a doll would strike us as childish, as undeveloped in a certain way. People generally grow out of feeling attached to dolls, blankets and the like. – But is this merely a fact about human development, a fact of 'natural history', in

Wittgenstein's phrase? If so, does that mean that 'Dolls don't feel
pain' is a conceptual truth only because, and to the extent that,
adults rather than children call the shots, including the linguistic
shots?

Surely not. Children don't differ from adults simply in virtue of
'having different feelings'. They know less, have less theoretical and
practical wisdom, see things (relatively speaking) through a glass
darkly, in ways that have quite definite, and familiar, consequences.
And of course it is only some, tender-hearted, children who get
upset about dolls. The feelings and responses of those who are less
wise themselves count as less wise. Feelings and responses of the
sort we are considering are not really separable from a person's
world-view, and they are susceptible to criticism as stemming from
a world-view which is susceptible to criticism.

This will have to go also, it seems to me, for what are often called
primitive cultures. To treat a tree as if it suffered – to fear the anger
of the thunder – these things are no more above criticism, or rather
above improvement, than are the tears of the child. One need not
make the mistake of regarding all religious language as proto-scien-
tific, or of neglecting ritualistic uses of language, in order to see
this.

Such cases as these may well be spoken of as ones in which certain natural responses are modified (or are modifiable) under the
influence of reason, in a broad sense of 'reason'. They are also cases
in which, with an increase in knowledge or wisdom, sympathy (or
something similar) will come to be withdrawn from some class of
objects – dolls or trees, for example. But, as mentioned in connection with children, the ways in which those less wise than us *are* less
wise have definite and familiar consequences. Children do not know
the ways of the world; their conception of death is often hazy; they
may err considerably about the needs and wants even of their
beloved pet animals ('I'm sure the goldfish would like to swim in
the *big* pond'). People in primitive cultures (of the sort at issue) may
believe that the health of crops depends on the performance of certain sacrifices – and so on. A person who has the usual protective
feelings towards a new-born baby, on the other hand, cannot be
called 'less wise' than a 'rationalist' who does not, or who tries not
to: such an assertion can have no content if there aren't any
consequences of unwisdom that can be pointed to, analogous to those
familiar to us from what children say and do.

In fact, reason and reflection are much more liable to lead to an
extension of sympathy than to a withdrawal of it. Perhaps the proper
name for the faculty in question, however, is 'imagination'. It is very
often an inability, or unwillingness, to imagine the details of real

cases that causes people to be callous. 'Imagining' can mean 'imagining what it's like' ('putting yourself in their shoes'), but certainly need not mean that. This is quite important, for the idea that sympathy derives always from 'imagining what it's like' (an idea to be found in writers as diverse as Rawls and Singer) tends to leave certain capacities for sympathy paralysed. After all, how can one imagine in any detail what it's like to be a new-born baby? Or a cat? Or a lunatic? One's imagination is inadequate to *these* tasks. But it is perfectly possible to imagine (and, of course, to witness) the suffering or pleasure of babies, cats and lunatics, and even of flies: 'And now look at a wriggling fly and at once these difficulties vanish and pain seems able to get a foothold here, where before everything was, so to speak, too smooth for it'.[11]

Everything is 'too smooth' so long as we try to attribute pain to something *on the model of* our own, or try to imagine what it's like to be that thing. One can, in the usual sense, imagine the pain of these creatures because one is capable of those natural reactions to others which form the basis of concepts like 'pain', and which we also feel, to some degree, towards whatever is sufficiently like a human being. The imagination feeds off such reactions, as well as off knowledge of how people and creatures do in fact behave. (Of course, our grasp of these concepts is *also* connected with our own capacities to feel pain, etc.)

As hinted at earlier, a society in which certain things are less often witnessed, or witnessed by fewer, will probably be one in which those things are less clearly imagined by many. In this context, pictures can bring knowledge: footage of war or famine, where it is not prurient, is valuable not only as documentary evidence, but because it is our reactions to the sorts of things depicted that enable us to judge the events in their moral and psychological aspects. The picture of a foetus can bring knowledge in the same way.

So far, our discussion has concentrated on people as objects of proper regard, sympathy, etc. When Locke described 'person' as a forensic term, he was thinking of agency and responsibility. In the domain of agency, we find that our natural responses to one another must still be accommodated.

'Cruelty has a Human Heart,
And Jealousy a Human Face;
Terror the Human Form Divine,
And Secrecy the Human Dress.'[12]

[11] Wittgenstein, *Philosophical Investigations*, par. 284.
[12] Part of William Blake's, 'A Divine Image', from *Songs of Experience*.

Why can't a tiger be really *cruel*? If we describe animals as 'cruel', this seems a sort of metaphor, though there are perhaps borderline cases: the cat which plays with the wounded mouse before despatching it, for example. A natural thing to say is that animals don't really have free will – they are driven by instinct. In which case, they surely aren't responsible for what they do.

It is not only animals who are let off the hook in this way. So are lunatics. How do these facts relate to our 'natural responses'?

In his paper 'Freedom and Resentment',[13] Strawson spoke of the natural reactions of resentment and gratitude as underlying our notions of responsibility, praise and blame; and he pointed out that these reactions are lacking, or are as it were neutralised, in certain cases. A harm done us may well produce no indignation or resentment if done accidentally, or by an animal, or by a small child, or by a pathologically unresponsive adult, such as an autist or psychopath. (Though it may in the last sort of case produce a response violent in its manifestation.)

Now one might ask whether this is just a 'brute fact': should we say, 'This is just how we feel about such cases'? A traditional philosopher may try to account for our attitudes to children, animals and psychopaths by saying that these are cases where freedom of will is lacking. Strawson is right, I think, in arguing that this gets things the wrong way round: the notion of freedom, far from having any connection with determinism or indeterminism (for example), has as its basis just those primitive reactions of resentment, etc., which we are examining, and (perhaps) trying to explain.

The fact that these reactions are primitive (having their origins in nature, not culture) doesn't mean that they are not modifiable through experience and reflection. We are back with the child and her doll. Perhaps a child can resent, and even try to punish, the misbehaviour of a pet budgerigar. But just as dolls don't feel pain, budgerigars are not responsible for their deeds. They know not what they do.

And this goes also for the pathologically unresponsive adult. But what do we mean by saying that a psychopath doesn't know what he is doing? Taken literally, it sounds absurd. He may well know that he is putting strychnine in someone's coffee, for instance; and he may well be able to predict the outcome of his actions.

If there is ignorance here, it is surely the ignorance of never having 'cottoned on'. Such cases are no doubt more complicated and subtle than my treatment of them may suggest; but it seems that there is at any rate a strong analogy with a conceptual lack. A blind person's grasp of colour-vocabulary is essentially parrot-like; a

[13] In Strawson's *Freedom and Resentment* (Methuen, 1974).

Roger Teichmann

tone-deaf person is deficient with concepts like 'octave'; a severe autist or psychopath will not have a full hold on psychological concepts. If everyone were psychopathic, such concepts would die out.

This means that arguing with a psychopath may well be futile. And it is this sort of fact which helps to explain the neutralising of feelings of resentment, etc. For such feelings, being the basis of a certain language-game, are themselves affected by obstacles to the conduct of that language-game – obstacles such as conceptual deficiency in another. One says of a psychopath, 'One can't get through to him'; and the communication that is at issue is both linguistic and emotional. In this way, our moral, psychological and linguistic reactions form a whole. They manage to do so, of course, largely because they are social reactions, reactions of social beings; they are not merely the pangs of an individual.

They are also primarily and paradigmatically reactions to fellow human beings. In a deliberate parallel with what was quoted above, Blake wrote:

> 'For Mercy has a human heart,
> Pity a human face,
> And Love the human form divine,
> And Peace, the human dress.'[14]

Without such human phenomena as mercy and pity, life would be nasty and brutish, if not short. These are human phenomena in that both those who feel them, and those who are the paradigm objects of them, are human beings.

[14] Part of Blake's, 'The Divine Image', from *Songs of Innocence*.

Just war

NICHOLAS DENYER

The innocent are immune. We must never, that is, make the object of any violent attack those who bear no responsibility for doing wrong to others; and only with grave reason and in extreme circumstances should we be prepared to cause them any incidental harm as we press home a violent attack against those who are its legitimate objects. This principle of the immunity of the innocent seems almost self-evidently true. This is not to say that the principle is incapable of further development and articulation, unsusceptible of marginal qualification, or underivable from deeper principles. It does however mean that any moral theory which denies this principle altogether will be something that only a fool or a knave could accept.

There is another principle, which I call the principle of the munity of the nocent. It holds that those who are (whether, as the phrase has it, 'morally', or perhaps 'just causally') responsible for doing wrong to others may rightfully be made the objects of violent attack. The munity of the nocent has an evidence almost equal to that of the immunity of the innocent. Few indeed even among pacifists would deny it; for in holding that those responsible for doing wrong to others *may* be rightfully attacked, it does not hold that anyone *must* participate in such an attack, much less that anyone may be rightfully compelled to do so.

An obvious place to apply these twin principles is warfare. The result would be that making war can sometimes be legitimate, but that there are strict limitations on the means that one may use even when waging a legitimate war. To be more precise, war may be waged against wrongdoers, but even in waging such a war one may attack only the wrongdoers themselves and not also or instead any innocent fellow countrymen, women or children of those wrongdoers.

These twin principles have often been applied to warfare with just this result. Indeed most medieval and early modern reflections on the legitimacy of warfare consist largely in working through the details of such an application.[1] Thus under the head of *ius ad bellum* they discuss the conditions under which one might rightfully go to war – who, that is, may wage war against which sorts of malefactor; and under the head of *ius in bello* they discuss the manner in which

---

[1] Frederick H. Russell, *The Just War in the Middle Ages* (Cambridge: Cambridge University Press, 1975) discusses the origins of this tradition.

war, once entered, might rightfully be waged – who, that is, is immune to which sorts of harm in virtue of which sort of innocence. And in this century too there are still those who attempt to deal with the morality of war in exactly this fashion. A prime example is Elizabeth Anscombe. In a justly celebrated series of papers[2] she follows this tradition in all save the vocabulary of *ius ad bellum* and *ius in bello*. Thus she argues that 'where there is no higher authority to which to appeal, as in the case of a sovereign state at war, men who are wrongfully attacking rights may be killed in order to defend those rights if they cannot be defended in any other way', adding almost immediately that 'no one may be deliberately attacked in war, unless his actions constitute an attack on the rights which are being defended or restored' (JPW, p. 77).

Anscombe however in these papers seems to be attempting more than simply a defence and application of our twin principles. For she seems at times to be attempting the further task of deriving from these principles, and defending on that basis, the law of war as we have it. This task, I will argue, is difficult, if not impossible: the law of war is not derivable from these principles, and in certain respects runs directly contrary to them. Yet, as I will argue also, the law of war cannot simply be rejected as immoral or ill-founded, for the law of war is better as it is than it would be were it modified to accord with our two compelling principles. The task then is as worthwhile as it is difficult, and in showing this I hope to detect and explain some weak spots in Anscombe's treatment of the topic. This leaves us with a paradox of sorts: how can we succeed where Anscombe has in part failed and reconcile our twin principles with the law of war as we have it? I will end this essay by hinting that the paradox yields to an anarchist and pacifist solution.

That there is a law of war should be less surprising than perhaps it is. Human beings characteristically structure their activities by all manner of rules, customs and institutions. Consider for instance how we deal with food and sex. It should be no surprise that we deal likewise with violence. And in any case violence needs a massive amount of institutionalisation – states (or something like them) with armies (or something like them) – even to begin to count as warfare. For large-scale violence needs thorough organisation. And even then, genocide and bloodily suppressed insurrections indicate that not all large-scale violence is war.

[2] 'War and Murder' (WAM), 'Mr Truman's Degree' (MTD) and 'The Justice of the Present War Examined' (JPW). References to these papers will be by abbreviated title and a page number of the reprints in G. E. M. Anscombe, *Collected Philosophical Papers*, Volume III: *Ethics, Religion and Politics* (Oxford: Basil Blackwell, 1981).

The law of war that I shall examine is that contained in the series of international treaties beginning with the 1865 Paris Declaration on Maritime Law.[3] These agreements themselves indicate that the law of war is not entirely their own creation. According to 1977 Geneva I, Art. 1, Para. 2, p. 390:

> In cases not covered by this Protocol or by other international agreements, civilians and combatants remain under the protection and authority of the principles of international law derived from established custom, from the principles of humanity and from the dictates of the public conscience.

The Preamble to 1907 Hague IV p. 45 is otherwise similar, save that it speaks of 'the usages established among *civilized* peoples' (my italics). Presumably however the signatories to 1977 Geneva meant to disallow the suggestion that any of them were uncivilised rather than to say that no custom of the civilised can count unless established among the uncivilised too. The consequence of all this is that the task of treaties has been not so much to create the law of war from nothing as to reaffirm, articulate, elaborate and clarify a law of war that enjoyed some existence independent of them. And because of this, a state which refuses to be a formal party to these agreements is not thereby freed from its obligations under the general principles that structure the international law of war; it is freed from at most the particular detail of the regulations in which these agreements embody those principles. To illustrate: Israel refuses to accept the provisions of 1949 Geneva I Art. 38, p. 185, regarding the display of the red cross, crescent, or lion and sun as an emblem of medical services, and says that it will display instead the Red Shield of David (Roberts and Guelph, p. 333). In making this reservation Israel is quite within its rights. No such reservation however could release Israel from its duty under international law to refrain from attacking duly marked medical services, or entitle Israel to claim immunity for any medical services of its own that are not displaying an appropriate emblem. Nor indeed does Israel suppose otherwise. In spite of this fact that the law of war enjoys some existence independent of explicit agreement, nevertheless the relevant treaties have come to be so widely ratified, and to cover so many aspects of warfare, that focussing my discussion on their provisions will not give a partial or lop-sided view of the international law of war.

[3] These agreements have been collected by Adam Roberts and Richard Guelff in *Documents on the Laws of War* (Oxford: Clarendon Press, 1982). I shall cite them by the date and place at which they were signed, where necessary by the number of the convention, article and paragraph referred to, and by a page number of Roberts and Guelff.

Nicholas Denyer

Ius ad bellum and *ius in bello* have received rather different treatments from international law. Modern international law has much to say about *how* one might rightfully wage war, and what it says does not always go altogether unheeded. It has however been far less successful in putting limits on *when* one might rightfully resort to war. To be more precise, it has had great success, but that success is more verbal than real. 'War' tends in some contexts to receive a very exacting definition: it is a legal state initiated by a declaration of war and terminated by a treaty of peace among the survivors. Furthermore, the stand that the Nuremberg Judgements and the United Nations Charter take against 'aggressive' wars, while too nebulous to have many further effects, nevertheless means that states are unwilling to incur the obloquy of initiating a war by declaring it. The upshot is that these days wars are rarely fought. What we have instead is 'armed conflict'; and that is as common as ever. The law that governs the waging of war has kept pace with this development. 1949 Geneva I, Art. 2, p. 171 declares that:

> the present convention shall apply to all cases of declared war or of any other armed conflict which may arise between two or more of the High Contracting Parties, even if the state of war is not recognised by one of them.

And twenty eight years later 1977 Geneva dropped 'war' from its vocabulary and spoke without further ado of 'armed conflicts'.

The reasons for this failure to effect more than a verbal change are not entirely discreditable. Cynics will rightly point out that the power to wage war more or less when one sees fit is traditionally an attribute of sovereignty; and that the sovereign powers whose agreement, whether express or tacit, determines the international law have been unwilling to divest themselves of this power. Nevertheless, no less important a factor in thwarting the development of *ius ad bellum*, of restrictions on the resort to war, has been the very development of *ius in bello*, of the international law that governs how war may be waged. This law is scrupulously impartial: the justice or otherwise of one's cause makes no difference whatsoever to what one may lawfully do in fighting for it. A recent provision which accords certain privileges to those 'fighting against colonial domination and alien occupation and against racist regimes in the exercise of their right of self-determination' (1977 Geneva I, Art. 1, Para. 4, p. 390) is sometimes cited as a so far isolated but very ominous exception to the impartiality of the law. In fact however it simply and not unreasonably says that wars in such a cause are to be treated as international armed conflicts, and it accords to those fighting for 'national liberation' no rights that it does not also accord to those fighting against. Not only is this body of law governing *ius in bello* itself quite impartial; it is also quite extensive, and so it simply leaves little or no room for provisions partial to those with right on their side. And this means: little or no room for any meaningful *ius ad bellum*.

Those responsible for the modern law of war have been well aware of this. They have noted that if any special licence to savagery is granted to those with right on their side then both belligerents will avail themselves of that licence; and they have noted similarly that if any special penalties are prescribed for those in the wrong then whichever side can inflict them will do so. For this reason humanitarians have joined with states in removing from the law of war traditional notions of just cause.[4] And they need not be ashamed of this achievement. For moralised war, war governed by principles which like the immunity of the innocent and the munity of the nocent are partial to those in the right, would certainly be no less savage, and probably be much more so, even than war as we know it.

Let us now turn to the area in which the law has burgeoned: the rightful waging of a war once entered. There is a similarity here between the modern law and that derivable from our twin principles. Our twin principles distinguish innocent from nocent, saying that the latter may, and the former may not, be made objects of violent attack. Similarly, modern law says that combatants may be attacked and that non-combatants may not. Furthermore both the modern law and our twin principles put in a similar qualification. Our twin principles go with a principle of double effect: while the innocent may never be the intended objects of a military attack, one need do no wrong if in an attack on a sufficiently large concentration of the nocent one incidentally kills a sufficiently small number of innocent bystanders. 'For', as Anscombe puts it, 'killing the innocent, even if you know as a matter of statistical certainty that the things you do involve it, is not necessarily murder' (MTD, p. 66). Representative principles from the international law are similar. Consider 1923 Hague Art. 24, p. 126:

> Aerial bombardment is legitimate only when directed at a military objective. ... In cases where [military objectives] are so situated that they cannot be bombarded without the indiscriminate bombardment of the civilian population, the aircraft must abstain from bombardment. In the immediate neighborhood of the operations of land forces, the bombardment of cities, towns, villages, dwellings or buildings is legitimate provided that there exists a

[4] See Geoffrey Best, *Humanity in Warfare: The Modern History of the International Law of Armed Conflicts*, 2nd. Edn (London: Methuen, 1983), pp. 44–5.

Nicholas Denyer

reasonable presumption that the military concentration is sufficiently important to justify such bombardment, having regard to the danger thus caused to the civilian population.

Here however the similarity between the law of war and our twin principles ends. For the distinction between nocent and innocent is not that between combatant and non-combatant. Nor furthermore do the roles that combatant and non-combatant play in the law of war correspond much to the roles of nocent and innocent under our twin principles.

Let me begin with the distinction between combatants and non-combatants. Combatants are defined by 1907 Hague IV, Annex, Art. 1, p. 48, as any group of people meeting the following conditions:

1 To be commanded by a person responsible for his subordinates;
2 To have a fixed distinctive emblem recognisable at a distance;
3 To carry arms openly; and
4 To conduct their operations in accordance with the laws and customs of war.

A long-standing qualification of this is the doctrine of *levée en masse*. In the wording of 1907 Hague IV, Annex, Art. 2, p. 48:

The inhabitants of a territory which has not been occupied, who, on the approach of the enemy, spontaneously take up arms to resist the invading troops without having had time to organise themselves in accordance with Article 1, shall be regarded as belligerents if they carry arms openly and if they respect the laws and customs of war.

A more recent qualification attempts to deal with guerrilla warfare. According to 1977 Geneva I, Art. 44, Para. 3, pp. 411–12:

Combatants are obliged to distinguish themselves from the civilian population while they are engaged in an attack or in a military operation preparatory to an attack. Recognising, however, that there are situations in armed conflicts where, owing to the nature of the hostilities, an armed combatant cannot so distinguish himself, he shall retain his status as a combatant, provided that, in such situations, he carried his arms openly:

(a) during each military engagement, and
(b) during such time as he is visible to the adversary while he is engaged in a military deployment preceding the launching of an attack in which he is to participate.

What these qualifications reveal is the essential element in the original definition of combatant. The thing that remains when all else fails is that to count as a combatant one must bear one's arms openly. It is then in a sense artifice that marks out combatants. A combatant is a combatant because he publicly shows himself as a combatant and so gains public acceptance as one. Customarily he shows himself as a combatant by wearing a uniform. But even where he does not avail himself of this conventional emblem, he must make an equivalent claim to, and demonstration of, his combatant status by carrying his arms openly.

There is a similar artifice in the marking out of certain non-combatants. One obvious example is the use of such emblems as the white flag to indicate surrendered troops, the red cross to indicate medical personnel, and the 'shield, pointed below, per saltire blue and white' (1954 Hague, Art. 16, p. 346) to indicate cultural property. International law requires not only the use of such emblems; it requires also wherever possible the geographical separation of anything that might properly be protected by them from any person or thing with combatant status and thus a proper object of attack. Representative are the provisions of 1954 Hague, Art. 8, p. 343:

> There may be placed under special protection a limited number of refuges intended to shelter movable cultural property... provided that they:
>
> > (a) are situated at an adequate distance from ... any important military objective...
> > (b) are not used for military purposes.

And without the artifice of geographical separation it is difficult if not impossible under international law to claim non-combatancy by using any of these emblems.

International law treats with great hostility anything that blurs the sharp line it tries to draw between combatants and non-combatants. One example of this is its attitude to armed forces sheltering behind the emblems whereby non-combatant immunity is conventionally claimed. Such behaviour is classed as 'perfidy' (e.g. 1977 Geneva I, Arts. 37, 38, pp. 409–10) and strictly forbidden. All steps feasible are taken to detect and punish violations of this prohibition. Under 1923 Hague Draft Rules, art. 27, Para. 8, p. 128, an inspection committee of neutrals was to check that a belligerent made no use of protected monuments or their environs for military purposes. A belligerent party himself, according to 1949 Geneva II, Art. 31, p. 204, 'shall have the right to control and search' hospital ships. And according to 1977 Geneva I, Art. 30, pp. 404–5, a belligerent may require a medical aircraft to land and be searched in order to establish that it is indeed a medical aircraft and no more. Any violations thus detected are to be punished in the obvious way, by denial of the claimed non-combatant immunity. Indeed, it seems that in certain cases punishment can go further: at any rate, there is no provision of international law whereby those who feign surrender in order to attack their enemy can expect to have their white flag respected a second time.

Another sign of the importance that international law lays on its distinction between combatants and non-combatants is its attitude to weaponry. Certain weapons are intrinsically incapable of respecting the distinction, and thus are ruled out. For example, under 1907 Hague VIII, Art. 1, p. 87:

It is forbidden –

1 To lay unanchored automatic contact mines, except when they are so constructed as to become harmless one hour at most after the person who laid them ceases to control them;
2 To lay anchored automatic contact mines which do not become harmless as soon as they have broken loose from their moorings;
3 To use torpedoes which do not become harmless when they have missed their mark.

On the same principle are forbidden also 'bacteriological methods of warfare' (1925 Geneva, p. 140) and 'environmental modification techniques' (1977 UN, Art. 1, p. 379). The same principle too, it should be noted, would rule out many, though not all, envisaged uses for nuclear weapons. And the fact that current technology is inconsistent with such an application of this principle would be of no moment if 1907 Hague VIII Art. 6, p. 88 is any precedent. For in that article, those parties not technologically capable of obeying the convention's rules undertook 'to convert the *matériel* of their mines as soon as possible' in order to become so.

We have now said enough to indicate three respects in which the distinction between combatants and non-combatants, on which the law of war places so much weight, differs from the Anscombe distinction between nocents and innocents.

Firstly, combatants are not distinguished from non-combatants by moral-cum-causal criteria: nothing about responsibility for wrong enters into the law's definitions of these notions. Likewise nocents are not distinguished from innocents by the artifices of conventional emblems and enforced geographical separation.

Secondly, the distinction between nocent and innocent is simply nowhere near as definite and as visible as the distinction that international law makes between combatant and non-combatant. Even in peace it can be hard to tell the difference between nocent and innocent; and especially in war all the gradations there can be of wrongdoing and responsibility for it will mean that in many cases there is no sharp difference to be told. Anscombe rightly points out that difficulties in borderline cases are no sound objection to a distinction between nocent and innocent (WAM, p. 59; MTD, p. 67). She does not however observe that the greater a distinction's failures in sharpness and visibility the less use it can have in a legal system. Nor does she observe that above all in the law of war, where the nice adjudication of civil life will obviously be impossible, the sharp and visible distinction of combatants from non-combatants is exactly what one needs.

Thirdly, there are of necessity combatants on both sides, whereas according to our twin principles there need be nocents only on one, the side without a just cause. Of course, as Anscombe points out, 'human pride, malice and cruelty are so usual that it is true to say that wars have mostly been mere wickedness on both sides' (WAM, p. 52). Nevertheless, she cannot use the pervasiveness of these vices to overthrow this distinction between nocents and combatants. For she is concerned to emphasise against pacifists that a just war is a real possibility (e.g. WAM, p. 55).

Let us now turn to what the international law makes of the distinction between combatant and non-combatant that it takes such pains to establish. Combatants may be attacked just as nocents may be attacked. But there the similarity ends. A combatant may be attacked only in such a way and to such an extent as to render him *hors de combat*. Thus he may be killed if need be, but even so there are limits. Dum-dum bullets (1899 Hague III, p. 40) and plastic shrapnel (1981 UN, Protocol I, p. 475) for example are forbidden as causes of gratuitous suffering. If you can get a bullet or a piece of shrapnel into your enemy, that is enough to put him out of action; so there can be no justification if you also make the bullet to expand and take a large chunk out of him, or make the shrapnel undetectable by X-rays and so irremovable save with the greatest of difficulty. It is not only from regulations about weapons that this idea may be illustrated. Surrendered soldiers (1907 Hague IV, Art. 23(c), p. 52), shipwrecked sailors (1949 Geneva II, Art. 12, pp. 198–9), and airmen parachuting from an aircraft in distress (1977 Geneva I, Art. 42, p. 411) are none of them proper objects of attack, for all are *hors de combat*. And the very article which protects parachuting airmen itself indicates that this is the rationale for the protection it accords them; for it adds 'Airborne troops are not protected by this Article'.

Such limitations are evidently desirable from all points of view. It is for example plain common sense to leave one's enemies with the option of a surrender after which no further harm will be done them. For those whose options are limited to death or glory are liable to go all out for the latter. By the same token of course one may well want one's own forces to *believe* they have no choice but death or glory, or want the enemy to believe that one's own forces have such a belief; nevertheless, for obvious reasons one must also want to retain in fact oneself the option of surrender. All parties then have strong motives to preserve a system whereby both they and their enemies can surrender without fear of further harm. (Which is probably why the procedures for surrender are so well entrenched a part of the international law.)

Anscombe acknowledges the desirability of these limitations on the violence that may be done to combatants. '[T]he enemy should not be attacked', she says (MTD, p. 67), 'more ferociously than is necessary to put them *hors de combat.*' Nevertheless, these limitations are not those that one would get by applying our twin principles of the immunity of the innocent and the munity of the nocent. The coercion that we apply, and rightly apply, to ordinary criminals is not limited to what is needed for their apprehension; it contains also a substantial punitive element. Why then may we not apply punitive coercion to those on whom we are justly making war, when the justice of our war against them hangs on the fact that they too are malefactors? Why should we be limited to putting them *hors de combat*?

Anscombe dismisses the answer that 'a man has no personal responsibility for fighting' (MTD, p. 67). And rightly so. It is of course true that one cannot be punished for wrongs one has done, if one did not know, and could not have been expected to know, that they were wrongs. It is true too that comparatively little knowledge can be expected of those under military discipline in time of war: a soldier ordered to shell a certain map reference cannot be expected to investigate carefully whether the spot contains a legitimate target. Nevertheless, these considerations fail to absolve all combatants from all blame. For they can absolve some combatants from the blame they would otherwise bear only by passing the buck to those higher up in the chain of command. What of other considerations? 'They are probably conscripts', for example? Or 'They were only led to volunteer by what their government told them'? No other consideration, it seems, could succeed where these have failed. For if any other consideration did have the effect that no combatant in an unjust cause could be blamed for fighting, it would be likely to have the untoward consequence that combatants on the right side too bore no responsibility, and thus could claim no credit. For the likelihood is that the consideration would be just as true of them as well.

Anscombe says instead that prisoners of war may not be tried and punished by their captors 'because they were not the subjects of the state whose prisoners they are' (MTD, p. 67). Her idea presumably is not that a state has jurisdiction only over its own nationals: for few courts would be impressed if a defendant pleaded foreign nationality. Perhaps then she intends some other sense of 'subject', whereby for example even a foreigner temporarily within the Queen's realms, and so enjoying her protection, is for the time being her subject. And Anscombe's unexpected change of tenses – '*were* not the subjects of the state whose prisoners they *are*' – may hint that prisoners are in this sense subjects of the states that hold them captive. Nevertheless, if prisoners are justly taken then they will, according to Anscombe, have been 'engaged in an objectively unjust proceeding which the [captor] *has the right to make his concern*' (WAM, p. 53; my italics). If their injustice was a legitimate concern of the captor state while they were not its subjects, why should it cease to be so subsequently? In particular, why should their injustice cease to be the captor's legitimate concern the moment that they do become its subjects?

If the liability of combatants to suffer violence is not exactly that of nocents, another feature of their status is in complete contrast to that assigned the nocent by our twin principles. Combatants not only may suffer violence; they also have the right to inflict it. Within the limits we have mentioned they may use all manner of violence, up to and including the infliction of violent death. And it is not only combatants in a just cause who have this right, but combatants in any. I say that combatants have such a right. I should be more clear. It is not that combatants have what Hohfeldians would call a claim right, for it is not wrong to prevent combatants from killing. Their opponents are after all entitled to do much, including kill them first, to prevent them exercising this right. The point is rather that combatants have a liberty right to kill: they do no wrong in killing.

Here it may help to employ the nice distinction that international law draws between 'judicial' and 'disciplinary' punishment (1949 Geneva III, Chapter III, pp. 249–58). The distinction is invoked in provisions dealing with the treatment of prisoners of war. Judicial punishment is punishment more or less as it is ordinarily understood: inflicting it denounces as wrong-doers those on whom it is inflicted. Disciplinary punishment is different. It conveys no suggestion of wrong-doing, and those subjected to it 'shall not in any case be transferred to penitentiary establishments (prisons, penitentiaries, convict prisons, etc.)' (1949 Geneva III, Art. 97, p. 253), that is, shall not be transferred to those places where wrong-doers undergo judicial punishment. Much that would in the ordinary course of events incur judicial punishment incurs no more than disciplinary punishment when committed by prisoners of war. In particular, as 1949 Geneva III, Art. 93, p. 252 has it:

> offences committed by prisoners of war with the sole intention of facilitating their escape and which do not entail any violence against life or limb, such as offences against public property, theft without intention of self-enrichment, the drawing up or use of false papers, or the wearing of civilian clothing, shall occasion disciplinary punishment only.

A prisoner of war may be made to suffer for his actions, even when, as is escape, they are part of his role as a soldier. But when they are, his sufferings can be no more than disciplinary. Similarly, the violence inflicted on soldiers in battle is no more than disciplinary: it does not deny their licence to do what the violence attempts to prevent.

Combatants have then a liberty right to use force. This follows from, indeed is but another way of stating, the limitations on the force that may be used against them. And just as the immunity of innocents and the munity of nocents could make no sense of those limitations, so too they can make no sense of the right. If our analogy is to be with the use of force by, say, the state against criminals, this right could belong to at most one side, and it would not be a liberty, but a claim right. Civil malefactors may not use violence to resist arrest; if they do, it only adds to their offences. And the police not only may use necessary force to apprehend wrong-doers, but also may not be forcibly interfered with in doing so.

Let us now turn to the difference between the status of the non-combatant under international law and that of the innocent under our twin principles. Non-combatant and innocent are alike in that neither may be made the object of attack. But a vital distinction remains. Non-combatants have no licence to use force. The penalty they pay for participating in war is loss of their non-combatant immunity. And this loss is not compensated for by any corresponding gain of combatants' rights. Thus the death penalty may after due trial be imposed upon civilians in occupied territory who have committed 'serious acts of sabotage against the military installations of the occupying power' (1949 Geneva IV, Art. 68, p. 294). In other words, non-combatants are subject to the ultimate judicial punishment should they do the very things for which combatants cannot even be tried, much less punished. And this of course applies regardless of the justice or otherwise of the cause in which they do these things.

This is not just an unfortunate feature of the current law to be modified at the next convention. No workable law of war could assign to innocents out of uniform any right to use force, while combining this right with an immunity from attack. For one cannot expect people at war to refrain from using force against those who might use force against them. It follows that if innocents out of uniform are to have such a right, they can have no such immunity. And a law of war which accorded innocents out of uniform no such immunity would be even less effective in constraining the horrors of warfare than the law of war as we have it. No legal licence to use force in war can then belong to innocents in general; it can belong only to those who carry their arms openly.

Can the twin principles of the immunity of the innocent and the munity of the nocent make sense of this? Under those two principles innocents may use force; indeed, only innocents may do so. If the immunity of non-combatants from attack depends on the fact that they are innocent, why then should they not be entitled to use force against combatants? In some cases no doubt the combatants whom they might attack are fighting justly in a just cause, and then it would be wrong for non-combatants to attack them. But it would be wrong for non-combatants to attack them, because it would be wrong for them to be attacked by anyone, combatants included. In other cases no doubt the strategy behind a 'non-combatant' attack on combatants will be that often adopted by guerrillas: to provoke an indiscriminate retaliation and so win over the wavering innocents who will be among its victims. Such an attack too would be wrong, for it is wrong to act with the intention that the innocent be harmed, even though the intention is that the harm be inflicted by others. But these cases do not exhaust the possibilities: there can be combatants in an unjust cause who can be attacked without the hope of thereby provoking them to an indiscriminate retaliation.[5] Why should civilians not join in such an attack? Why should they have to put on a uniform or otherwise 'carry their arms openly' before doing so? If nothing else, fairness seems to forbid civilians to take part in hostilities: if they want to be immune from force they shouldn't use it themselves. It seems furthermore particularly indecent to use one's civilian status as camouflage in order to make an attack that will depend for its success on the enemy's willingness to respect non-combatant immunity. And in any case such indecency

[5] One instance is reported from 1940's France in Michael Walzer, *Just and Unjust Wars: A Moral Argument with Historical Illustrations* (Harmondsworth: Penguin, 1980), p. 176.

Nicholas Denyer

is quite unnecessary, for an enemy who can be defeated only by his respect for non-combatants is not one whose victory would be an unmitigated disaster. None of this however can make much sense under our twin principles. For if our analogy is to be with the use of force against criminals we should recollect that it is legitimate to have citizens' arrest and plain clothes policemen.

The difference between innocents and non-combatants is therefore as large as the difference between combatants and nocents. And these differences are systematically connected. A combatant has the innocent's right to attack and the nocent's liability to be attacked; whereas a non-combatant has the nocent's duty to refrain from attacking and the innocent's immunity from being attacked. These four ingredients – the right, the liability, the duty and the immunity – are parcelled out in one way by our twin principles, and in another by the international law of war. And for all the plausibility of our twin principles, one could not expect the law of war to parcel out these four ingredients in any way other than it does.

There is one clear corollary of all this. It concerns Anscombe's refutation of pacifism. The 'doctrine of pacifism' which she defined as 'It is *eo ipso* wrong to fight in wars' (WAM, p. 55), is proclaimed false on the grounds that violence against wrongdoers is permissible (WAM, pp. 51–2). But warfare, we have seen, is not just any kind of violence. It has a structure and a code of its own, a structure and a code underivable from the compelling pair of moral principles with which we began. In this it is like duelling, or prize-fighting. And just as duelling or prize-fighting cannot be legitimated by appeal to the fact that violence is not as such impermissible, so too one can consistently call it *eo ipso* wrong to fight in wars while acknowledging it legitimate for police to fight against malefactors.[6]

Though this is clear, the rest is obscure. Above all, it is obscure how to square our two compelling principles with the fact that the law of war had better remain as it is. Perhaps this pacifist answer deserves further investigation: Our twin principles need no modification to cope with warfare. They can be allowed to stand, and so they will rule out war as an immoral institution. The validity that belongs to the law of war is that which belonged to the law of duelling. So long as there was an aristocracy, whose members had the power to conduct disputes between themselves by force, it was as well for there to be the institution of duelling, to channel and limit the damage done. For merely forbidding such a conduct of

---

[6] Jenny Teichman, 'Pacifism', *Philosophical Investigations*, Volume V, 1980, pp. 72–83, gives sound arguments to show how war differs from policing.

disputes did not and could not achieve anything while there remained an aristocracy with that power. Likewise, it achieves nothing simply to forbid violence between states. Better then that their violence be channelled and limited by the law of war. With duelling, it proved in the end best of all to have none of it, and that meant no aristocracy either. Likewise with war: the best course of all may be to abolish war itself, and therefore abolish with it those institutions whose violence creates the need for a law of war. That would require either one world state, or else no states whatsoever.[7]

[7] Numerous gatherings in Cambridge and Perth have heard earlier versions of this paper. Professor Anscombe was present at one of these gatherings, and she has read a written version too. The kind and courteous comments of all concerned, and not least of Professor Anscombe herself, call for much gratitude.

Index of Names

Index of Names